Computer Applications in Language Learning

Theo Bongaerts, Pieter de Haan,
Sylvia Lobbe and Herman Wekker (eds.)

Computer Applications in Language Learning

1988
FORIS PUBLICATIONS
Dordrecht - Holland/Providence RI - U.S.A.

Published by:
Foris Publications Holland
P.O. Box 509
3300 AM Dordrecht, The Netherlands

Distributor for the U.S.A. and Canada:
Foris Publications USA, Inc.
P.O. Box 5904
Providence RI 02903
U.S.A.

CIP-data

Computer

Computer Application in Language Learning / Theo Bongaerts (eds.) ... [et al.] - Dordrecht [etc.] : Foris
ISBN 90 6765 400 0 (Paper)
SISO 455.4 UDC 681.3:372.88
Subject heading: computer applications in language learning

ISBN 90 6765 400 0 (Paper)

Printed in The Netherlands by ICG Printing, Dordrecht.

CONTENTS

Preface vii

Sylvia Lobbe and Marlies Smit
CALL in the Netherlands 1

Tim Johns
Whence and Whither Classroom Concordancing 9

David Hardisty
Lessons from the Classroom 35

Frank van Ruysselvelt
The Computer across the Curriculum: English and Information Technology 47

Scott Windeatt
The Use of Word Processors in Language Teaching 57

Albert Sleutjes
Coherence in CALL Software 71

Paul Looijmans and Carla Seifert
Applying ALEXIS in Foreign Language Teaching: How to Develop a Feedback Database 75

Joseph Rézeau
CALL and the integrated Professional Package FRAMEWORK 87

James Pankhurst
Recent Experiences in Large-Scale Computer-Assisted Instruction 107

Luice Huiskens and Peter-Arno Coppen
ZICOM: An Application of the Authoring System AMOR 117

Nico Robat
On Developing a Sentence Analysis Program: A Progress Report 135

Hans van Halteren
Possible Uses of Syntactic Analysis Trees in Syntax Teaching 147

Software list 163

Author Index 167

List of Contributors 169

Preface

This volume contains a selection of the papers read at two international CALL conferences held in the Netherlands in the year 1987 (CALL is the acronym for Computer-Assisted Language Learning). The first conference took place at the University of Nijmegen on 23 January, and the second at the Teacher Training College Zuidwest Nederland in Delft on 5, 6 and 7 March 1987. In both cases the theme of the conference was the use of the computer in English language learning, and the audiences consisted largely of teachers in secondary and tertiary education, publishers and school administrators. The emphasis at both conferences was clearly on the practical application of computers in foreign language learning.

There is a growing interest in the Netherlands in the use of microcomputers in language learning. In the past few years the Dutch Ministries of Education and Economic Affairs have set up fairly large-scale projects to stimulate the introduction of computers into secondary schools. These projects, partly sponsored by computer firms, enable teachers to attend in-service training courses in the use of computers and assist them in introducing the computer into the school curriculum. Teachers have become much more aware of what use can be made of the new technology and what software is currently available for the subjects they teach. It is against this background of increasing interest in computer assisted learning that the conferences in Nijmegen and Delft were organized by the English Departments there. And it is not surprising that both occasions should have attracted large numbers of participants.

This book is intended to stimulate the interest in the use of the computer in language learning, and to contribute to the development of CALL software.

Our thanks are due to Henk Barkema and Henk la Roi for preparing the manuscript for this book.

TB
PdH
SL
HW

CALL in the Netherlands

Sylvia Lobbe
Marlies Smit

0. INTRODUCTION

In the last ten years there has been a rapidly growing interest in the use of computers in schools. First it was usually the science teachers who became aware of the advantages of the computer and later they even started to develop programs for other subjects than their own. The past few years language teachers have also begun to examine the possibilities computers have to offer. Several small-scale projects were set up on different types of computers. Schoolteachers tried to develop software without the help of professional programmers. This has typically resulted in a number of small, usually dedicated programs, which can only be used by schools that happen to have the same computers.

With the growing enthusiasm for computers the need for software has also increased enormously. The lack of educational software which is generally available and the large variety of hardware have slowed down the integration of the computer into the school curricula.

Therefore in order to stimulate the introduction of the computer into the Dutch secondary schools and the development of educational software, a number of projects have been set up. At the same time a plan for in-service training courses was developed. The aim of these courses is to familiarize teachers with the new technology. It should be noted, however, that the interest in the computer as a medium of instruction has by no means been restricted to secondary education. As can be concluded from the papers on computer applications in language learning in tertiary education collected in this volume, teachers in universities and teacher training colleges have also begun to realize the educational potential of the computer.

In the present article we shall give a brief description of the main projects which were set up in the Netherlands to stimulate the use of the computer in schools. Next we will briefly describe the in-service training course which is being developed specifically for language teachers. Finally, the papers in this volume, which are based on presentations at the Nijmegen conference on the computer in English language learning and the CALL conference in Delft, will be introduced.

1. THE MAIN PROJECTS

1.1 The NIVO project

In 1984 the Dutch Ministry of Education set up a project to stimulate the introduction of computers into secondary schools. This project is called the Information Technology Stimulation Plan (INSP); it will finish in 1989. One of the main stumbling blocks at the time was the diversity of computers being used in schools. Therefore another project was set up, the NIVO project (New Information Technology for Secondary Education). It is a joint venture on the part of the Ministries of Education and Economic Affairs and three computer firms: IBM, Tulip and Philips. The computer firms supply the hardware; the Ministry of Education is responsible for the in-service training courses for teachers; the Ministry of Economic Affairs gives financial support.

The NIVO project tries to ensure that all Dutch schools providing secondary education have 10 IBM compatible 16-bit computers at their disposal. Moreover, the project makes provision for three teachers from every school involved to follow a course of training in the use of computers. Apart from this basic training course a number of subject-specific courses are being organized as well to help teachers to introduce the computer into the curriculum for their subject and to give them an idea of the software which is available at the moment.

What changes has the NIVO scheme brought about so far? First of all, the universities and colleges of education have begun to introduce the computer into their teaching programs in various ways. Many of the language departments now have a course component in which students are introduced to various computer programs and ways of using them in the classroom. In their own curricula computer programs are used for exercises in syntax and for vocabulary testing. There is as yet no widespread or integrated use of the computer in the training of writing skills.

Various institutes are involved in the production of computer programs or content material for authoring programs. Especially the need for sufficient high quality material for the subject-specific in-service training courses has led to a number of projects being set up to produce these programs.

1.2 The IBM-SCO project

In 1983, a year before the INSP started, the IBM-SCO project was set up. In close cooperation with schoolteachers in North and South Holland, and various departments of the University of Amsterdam, the SCO (Centre for Educational Research) has produced some 20 programs for mathematics,

Dutch and computer science. The computer science programs show how the computer can be integrated into other subjects. The mathematics and language programs are reteaching programs, i.e. they can be used to brush up the knowledge the pupils acquired at primary school. The best known program is 'Schatten', in which the pupils have to guess e.g. the distance between two objects, the height of bridges and towers, time between the flashes of a lighthouse and find the treasure. Both these activities are implied in the Dutch pun 'schatten'.

Under the auspices of the INSP, SCO has started two new projects for mathematics and English. The English project is a joint venture between the English department of the University of Amsterdam and the English department of the College of Education in Delft.

1.3 The IBM-OMO project

In the same year the IBM-OMO project was set up. Programs for sentence analysis and arithmetics have been produced. In a follow-up project Discatexte has been developed. This is a reading comprehension program which has been set up to help students who have done five or six years of French to understand exam texts. It provides help at word, sentence and paragraph level, and gives information about words, sentence structure and grammar. The idea of producing a similar program for English is being studied.

1.4 The EEC project

With the help of EEC money a program is under development at COI (Centre for Education and Information technology) in Enschede that will allow teachers and pupils to enter their own texts and create a great number of activities around them. The system includes a word processor, a gapfilling generator and a wordbank. The gapfilling generator offers a great number of possibilities: e.g. free gaps, cloze tests, multiple-choice answers, matching. The wordbank is not meant to be used as a dictionary; it allows pupils and teachers to enter words with semantic fields and personal associations as definitions. The system is to be tested in Denmark, England and the Netherlands, starting in June 1988.

1.5 The POCO project

The follow-up of the NIVO project, as far as courseware development is concerned, is the POCO project (Courseware Development for Computers in Education), which was set up by the Dutch Ministry of Education in 1987. The purpose of the project is to produce software geared to the existing curricula for the various subjects. A number of courseware groups have started; one of them is making material for English in secondary schools.

Cooperation with the educational publishing houses should ensure the suitability of the contents.

2. THE IN-SERVICE TRAINING COURSE FOR FOREIGN LANGUAGE TEACHERS

Part of the NIVO project is the training of secondary school teachers in the use of the computer in their own subject. In-service training courses are being set up which introduce teachers to the software that is available for their subject and give them insight into the ways the software can be used.

For foreign language teachers at secondary schools the course will consist of a number of modules. Per module programs will be shown which can be used for training in a particular skill.

Both dedicated software and authoring systems will be included and their pros and cons discussed. In the long run authoring systems may prove to be more useful because they are more flexible. But however good an authoring system or dedicated program may be, it takes a lot of time to select and adapt good classroom material or to integrate it into the lessons. Therefore various ways of using the programs in class will be discussed and where possible tried out. At the same time it will be shown how the computer may help to do away with the artificial barriers between productive and receptive skills.

3. THE PAPERS

The papers presented at the conferences held in Delft and Nijmegen in 1987 are largely practical in their approach. On the one hand they suggest and describe uses of the computer and software in various teaching situations ranging from secondary schools to universities, and try to point the way to further developments which might prove beneficial; on the other hand they describe the development of software with the help of the available tools and the development of new systems.

Computers should and can be used in language teaching as an extra tool. They enable teachers and learners to work in accordance with the latest insights gained from research into the way people learn foreign languages. In recent years researchers seem more and more convinced that language teaching and learning is more efficient if the curriculum is styled to suit the learners' needs, and if the learners are given greater responsibility for their learning process. As in first language acquisition, the formation and testing of hypotheses, i.e. discovery learning, is seen as one of the basic strategies in acquiring competence in a foreign language.

An environment which provides the learners with ample material and which gives them the freedom for this type of discovery learning is hard to create in a traditional classroom setting with its prescribed curriculum and material. Those involved in CALL do see ways to put more tailor-made, independent learning into practice by using the unique opportunities the computer offers. If this approach is adopted, it will involve drastic changes in traditional classroom settings and obviously such changes will have to be gradual and its results and consequences carefully monitored.

The contributions in this volume reflect this attitude. They describe programs and strategies that will allow teachers to give their students more freedom and a wider choice in learning strategies.

The paper by Johns on the use of concordancing in classrooms is a good example of how students can be given greater responsibility for their learning and the shift this involves in the traditional teacher/learner roles. The teacher becomes a person who manages small-scale language research, the learner is the one who carries it out. Together they examine texts and discover facts that cannot always be easily found in grammar books or dictionaries. An example Johns gives is the difference between 'therefore' and 'hence'. The dictionaries consulted give unhelpful definitions. John's concordance, however, shows that there are subtle differences in usage. With the concordance program learners can try to discover rules for themselves. The teacher provides the texts or, alternatively, makes exercises based on the printout of the concordance. One example is an exercise where the target item has been blanked out and the learners have to guess the item with the help of the context sentences given.

According to Hardisty, information transfer and processing are at the heart of both information processing (the way the computer is used outside the classroom) and communicative methodological principles. The way CALL is used reflects these principles. Hardisty gives a number of practical examples and discusses choices that have to be made: should a weaker learner get remedial help from a computer program, while the other learners work with the teacher or should it be the other way around? Shouldn't the weaker learner get the advantage of getting special attention from the expert, the teacher?

At the Teacher Training College in Sittard a deliberate choice was made for the use of commercial packages in situations closely resembling real life. Van Ruyssevelt shows how simulation can be used to illustrate how information technology functions in the outside world. He gives the example of his students using data gathered through electronic mail as the basis for newssheets. They learn to work with professional word processing programs and set up databases that can be used in teacher training.

In Windeatt's paper we find many examples of the practical uses of the word processor. Students make summaries, take notes or expand their notes. They rewrite texts so that e.g. a descriptive text is made into a series of instructions or vice versa. He also describes how writing can be used as a preparation for reading. Students get a rough outline of a story and write their own version of it before they read the story itself. Ideas developed around word processing are universal in that they can be used with any word processing program unless special facilities are required, like mail merge.

Sleutjes expresses the need for simpler 'dedicated' programs allowing teachers direct use without adaptations. At the same time criteria for choosing such software are discussed. Too many of the currently available programs are isolated examples of CALL techniques rather than coherent pieces of software.

Looymans and Seifert give a description of the ALEXIS program which provides teachers with a consistent and versatile tool for feedback to students. Its main program contains a database of feedback texts. The teacher gives the numbers of the comments he wants to give and the feedback texts are put in a feedback report which is given to the learner. The program was originally developed for the correction of Dutch papers. But because it is basically an 'empty shell' program, databases can be set up for other subjects. The paper discusses the creation of this type of feedback database. A number of questions are discussed: Should the focus be on errors or on good and bad points? How should errors be classified? How elaborate should the feedback texts be? At the moment there are plans to set up an ALEXIS database for English.

Using FRAMEWORK, an integrated professional package developed for MS-DOS computers, Rézeau has been making material for his own pupils. In his paper he gives a number of practical examples of exercises which can be used directly in the classroom. He describes text manipulation exercises, mazes and automatic text generation and how he uses them in his teaching. Like Johns he has developed a concordance program, which he and his pupils use to study e.g. differences between the mother tongue and the foreign language.

Pankhurst too describes the use of a tool in producing material. He has been using the authoring package TAIGA for the preparation of a course of English grammar for students at the University of Utrecht. In his paper he gives a description of the process of producing CALL software. As he had no experience in developing software, he had to start from scratch. He gives an account of the decisions that had to be taken and the problems encountered during the production of the courseware. He also includes a discussion of the students' reactions and how these have helped to shape the exercises.

Huiskens and Coppen give an introduction to the AMOR authoring system with which interactive exercises can be made for any subject and discuss an application of this system called ZICOM. This program has been developed for the teaching of sentence analysis at the University of Nijmegen. Its aim is to help students gain insights into sentence structure and develop strategies that will enable them to analyse sentences. The program consists of a network of questions and follow-up questions that are triggered off when the students give incorrect or partially correct answers. Feedback and follow-up questions should put the students on the right track again.

Robat reports on the development of a small-scale sentence analysis program as part of a computer-assisted instruction project aimed at exploring the possibility of incorporating CAI/CALL into the curriculum at the University of Groningen. The program for sentence analysis consists of two text files that contain analysed sentences, information and help options. These files can be edited by means of a word processor. The efforts needed to translate classroom practice into a computer program prove to be enormous. So far a computer program has been developed that offers students additional or remedial training in function labelling. A program for class labelling is in the process of being produced.

Sentence analysis is also the topic of Van Halteren's paper. He discusses the possible applications of a linguistic database for the teaching of sentence analysis. The database, developed at the University of Nijmegen, was originally set up for linguistic research. It contains a large number of syntactic analysis trees. As it proved flexible and easy to use, it was felt that it could be used as a basis for an exercising tool. This practical component called CLUES is now being developed for tertiary level. Various types of exercises have been made: the student has to give the label of a given node in an analysis tree, find the nodes that have a particular label or indicate an example of a combination of labels. Because the program itself determines which sentences are going to be used in an exercise, there are a number of problems concerning student feedback. Still it is hoped that the program can be tried out in the second year syntax course for students of English in 1988.

4. CONCLUSION

Ten years ago few teachers were interested in computers and computer-assisted language learning. It is therefore remarkable that so many teachers, especially at teacher training colleges and universities, are now exploring the possibilities computers have to offer language teachers in the Netherlands.

The NIVO project has aroused a lot of interest, also on the part of language teachers. The two conferences whose proceedings are outlined in this volume were organized because of this growing interest. Teachers and researchers were given a chance to become acquainted with the work that is being carried out in the field of computer-assisted language learning and language research.

At the moment the software and hardware available is too limited to have a real impact on the way languages are taught. However, it is a good sign that both in the training courses and the development schemes the emphasis is on integration and a creative approach to the use of the computer rather than on practice and drill. Whether or not the computer is going to change the daily practice of language teaching and language learning will depend largely on the teacher training schemes and the opportunities given to teachers to explore this new medium.

Whence and Whither Classroom Concordancing?

Tim Johns

0. INTRODUCTION

A concordancer is a computer program that is able to search rapidly through large quantities of text for a target item (morpheme, word or phrase) and print out all the examples it finds with the contexts in which they appear (see figs 1-6 in the appendix). In this paper I shall outline the background to, and current developments in, work using an interactive concordancer in the classroom (Johns 1986), and suggest certain directions that work may take in future.[1]

1. ASSUMPTIONS

In talking about and demonstrating a simple concordancer (Micro-Concord Mark I) for the Sinclair Spectrum over the past couple of years, I have noticed that the program tends to divide language teachers into two camps. Some have reacted with enthusiasm, a few going so far as to write and try out their own versions of the program, often with interesting extensions and improvements that I have not hesitated to 'borrow back'. Other have been puzzled by it: while ready to concede that access to the facts of the language afforded by a concordancer may be of use to researchers, materials writers and teachers, they have failed to see that it could be of any use to a learner - or at any rate to a learner below the most advanced level. This division has little to do with language teachers' alleged fear of computer technology, and a great deal to do with underlying assumptions about the nature of language learning and the role of the teacher in that process. For that reason, I shall start by stating three basic assumptions that arise from my experience as a service teacher of English to overseas postgraduate students in a wide range of subject areas at Birmingham University, and indicate what I believe to be their relevance to CALL in general and their particular application to classroom concordancing.

1.1 The learner's engagement

The first assumption is that text (both spoken and written) and the learner's engagement with text should play a central role in the learning process. In that engagement, a key concept is that of authenticity, viewed from three points of view – authenticity of script, authenticity of purpose, and authenticity of activity. The most obvious of these is authenticity of script. The use of unsimplified texts with learners does not, of course, mean that the traditional helping role of the teacher is withdrawn: rather, it is transferred from the stage of text preparation to the stage of text presentation, the teacher helping learners to explore the limits of what they can discover at their individual level of ability. That approach can, of course, present difficulties if students believe or have been led to believe that to understand *anything* they should understand *everything*. By authenticity of purpose I mean that the text should be of value to the learner quite apart from its use in a language-teaching context, and that the part played by the teacher should be to help to make that value available to the learner. Here most teachers have to play a game of make-believe with their students: 'Let us read this text *as if you had* to find the salient facts/write a summary/learn how to imitate it ...'. In our work we are fortunate that we can often get the students to identify and provide the texts that they are having to work with on their courses or in their research, and to base our work on what they and their subject teachers tell us they have to do with those texts. In that situation, *as if you had* is replaced by *because you have*. The third concept – authenticity of activity – implies that what is done with the text should be transferable to the situation outside the classroom where the learner is trying to make sense of the language without the help of the teacher or of teaching materials. From this point of view, multiple-choice questions and other quiz-like activities seem to have low transferability, while others such as task reading and diagramming of text have high transferability (Johns and Davies, 1983).

To suggest that quizzes may have low transferability is not to deny their popularity with learners: in discussions of CALL, for example, it has been noted that when students have free choice among a range of different programs it is often the quizzes and drills that are most frequently chosen. Many plausible explanations can be put forward for this phenomenon. The quiz-like structure of many language tests encourages learners to identify mastery of the quiz with knowledge of the language. The familiarity and the simplicity of the format are attractive – and also, perhaps, its very artificiality since here everything is reduced to a simple choice between 'right' and 'wrong', in contrast with the confusing complexities of choice in the real world. The computer adds to the attraction, since it gives the learner immediate feedback and the chance to 'have another go' until the quiz is mastered. Inasmuch as the quiz can increase motivation and self-confidence ('I now know that I know') it clearly is of value: what is not so clear is how far doing multiple-choice questions on a text, say, can help learners to develop appropriate reading strategies that can be applied outside the classroom. On a historical note, it was this concern with text and with authenticity broadly understood that was the starting-point for my first experiments with text manipulation and text reconstruction on the University mainframe computer in the summer of 1980 (Johns 1981). At first sight the activities involved (reconstructing a paragraph in which the sentences have been jumbled, for example, or one in which all the words have been blanked out) do not appear to be particularly authentic, and are not in the sense that this is something which learners commonly have to do away from the computer or outside the classroom. Nevertheless, it did seem to me at the time that this was a transferable activity in the sense that piecing together coherent text from disconnected ideas or minimal clues lies very close to the heart of language learning and language use, while it retains the element of challenge that makes the quiz so popular. The subsequent development of the 'British School of CALL' in which text reconstruction programs have played a central role (John Higgins' STORYBOARD and Bob Moy's TRAY being the best-known examples) has confirmed that early intuition.

1.2 The teacher's behaviour

The second assumption is that the effectiveness of the teacher is potentially greatest when he or she is most at risk. An extreme example of minimum risk is the scenario in which the teacher ploughs through a textbook reading out the explanations and checking students' answers to exercises against the teacher's key. In many countries this is the expected behaviour on the part of teachers, who will assume that any alternative behaviour will lead to loss of respect from their students: it is also the behaviour to be expected when the teacher's own command of the foreign language is insecure. Even within that scenario a situation of high risk may arise if a student has the temerity to ask a question: 'Please, what is the difference between *therefore* and *hence*?' Here even the experienced native speaker may be unable to provide an adequate explanation or illustration of the point requested, and an opportunity for genuine teaching and learning will be missed. What often happens in practice, of course, is that teachers develop strategies for avoiding risk by evading questions, and in so doing suppress the innate curiosity that is a precondition – perhaps the precondition – for successful language learning (Smith 1975).

An example of an approach involving a deliberate courting of risk on the part of the teacher as well as all three aspects of authenticity outlined above is provided by our work in team-teaching on post-experience MSc courses in Transportation and Highway Engineering and in the Conservation of Plant Genetic Resources, where during the first term's work we tape-record lectures in the departments concerned, and having written an 'ephemeral' teaching handout on the basis of the recording, a day or so later check understanding of the lecture at various levels (overall structure of argument, applications and implications, points of linguistic difficulty, in particular the features of 'colloquial technical' language), the subject teacher who gave the lecture always being present and taking part in the session (see Johns and Dudley-Evans (1979) for a fuller description of this work). The element of risk in this situation – the possibility we may fail to understand or respond adequately to the lecture – gives every team-teaching session a tang of the unpredictable that is probably its most valuable feature: we are, so to speak, placing ourselves alongside our students in attempting to solve the communicative tasks that face them, and thereby often find that we gain insights, otherwise inaccessible, that put us on a firmer footing when preparing common-core materials for students across a range of different subject areas.

In relation to CALL generally, it is worth noting that many programs go out of their way to emulate the most risk-avoiding teacher imaginable and in that role can be more patient and more accurate and more stupid than any human teacher could contrive to be: from that point of view it is the teacher who most sedulously avoids risk who is, in fact, in the greatest danger of being supplanted by the new technology. The question remains whether that role is the only or the most appropriate one, either for the human being or the machine. Among the many alternative approaches, two in particular are worth considering here, both of which involve reversing the flow of question and answer and allowing the learner to interrogate the machine. The first is that we allow the computer itself to take risks by offering an inevitably limited, and potentially fallible, 'expert system' that will attempt to respond intelligently to student queries (see, for example, the program LOAN in Higgins and Johns 1984). The further development of that approach is to a large extent dependent on research in artificial intelligence as applied to natural language. The second approach – which for the immediate future appears to be more promising – is to offer tools that will allow the teacher and the learner to take risks more effectively, and where the intelligence involved is that of the human user. This second approach – based more on database than upon AI techniques – is the one taken by the work reported on in this paper.

1.3 The nature of language learning

The third assumption has to do with the nature of language learning.

One way of approaching this large topic is by considering the metaphors for learning that appear to underlie the various activities that teachers undertake with learners in classrooms. Where the emphasis is on tasks such as the rote learning of rules, verb paradigms, vocabulary lists and so forth, the metaphor would appear to be that of the hypodermic syringe: language learning requires the *injection* or *insertion* of knowledge. Another view of language learning sees it as a branch of gymnastics: by the use of carefully controlled *exercises* and *drills* (notice how both terms spell out the metaphor explicitly), the learner will gradually accumulate complex language *skills* (again metaphorical – see Phillips (1986) for a perceptive discussion of the dangers in the context of CALL of taking the metaphor too literally). Yet another metaphor sees language learning as a swimming pool requiring the *total immersion* of the learner in the foreign language, the role of the teacher being that of a swimming pool attendant ready to throw a life belt to anyone in danger of drowning. It is not my purpose here to discuss in detail the arguments for and against these views of the language learning process, but two general points may be worth making. The first is that reasoned eclecticism is a perfectly tenable theoretical position, and in practice there may be no great harm in mixing metaphors: at different times and for different purposes I attempt to inject, to exercise, and to immerse my students. The second general point is that the (first) acceptance of a particular metaphor is dependent not only on the social, cultural and political setting of a particular society at a particular point in time and the development of education within that setting but also on the technology available in the classroom. The technology of the slate which had to be wiped clean at the end of every lesson inevitably led to an emphasis on rote learning. Kelly (1969:260-1) has pointed out that the widespread adoption by the middle of the nineteenth century of grammar translation methods (the first to use exercises extensively) would have been impossible without the steam printing press which for the first time made it possible to assume that all pupils in a class would have copies of the same cheap textbook and could be working on the same material simultaneously. During the Cultural Revolution many Chinese managed to keep in touch with the outside world through the technology of the transistor radio, listening clandestinely to the BBC and the Voice of America: a form of immersion learning so effective that when entrance to universities was again opened up to competitive examination in 1977-8 the level of English of the new students was often far higher than that of their teachers, and elderly professors had to be brought out of retirement to teach them. In the context of the present paper it is worth speculating whether the new technology of the 1980's will make available a new metaphor for language learning, and how that metaphor might be realised in practice.

One candidate for the metaphor of the computer age has, in fact, already been around for some time as a variant of the immersion metaphor, and suggests that the closest parallel for language learning is with linguistic research (Seliger 1983). Like a researcher, the learner has to form preliminary hypotheses on the basis of intuition or scanty evidence: those hypotheses then have to be tested and rejected or refined against further evidence, and finally integrated within an overall model. The metaphor is consistent with the post-Chomskyan view of first language learning, and also with much that has been written about 'natural' second language learning outside the classroom (Dulay and Burt 1978). In the story of 'Shanace and the Passive' the metaphor lies at the heart of the late Julian Dakin's seminal book *The Language Laboratory and Language Learning* (1973:14-15), and it is implicit in many methodological innovations and rediscoveries of recent years – for example those various activities which are loosely gathered together under the heading of *discovery learning.* It is, moreover, a metaphor readily grasped by the majority of my students, who are familiar with research methods across a number of different disciplines, and are used to looking for underlying patterns and regularities in data that on first inspection appear confused and irregular.

If taken seriously the research metaphor carries with it certain consequences. Firstly, it entails a shift in the traditional division of roles between student and teacher, with the student now taking on more responsibility for his or her learning, and the teacher acting as research director and research collaborator rather than transmitter of knowledge. Secondly, it implies a greater degree of awareness of language and how language operates on the part of the learner than would be allowed in behaviourist models of language learning. Thirdly, it is crucial that the insights gained through research activities should not remain at the level of 'knowing about' the language, but should have direct pay-off in terms of use of the language and ability to communicate in it. And fourthly, it requires that the learner have available appropriate research tools. One of the problems in language learning is that in the early stages one's attention is focussed on high-frequency items and it is not difficult to find a number of examples of a particular word or structure to confirm or disconfirm a preliminary hypothesis: Shanace was able to revise her first guess at what the difference might be between active and passive sentences because she was listening to a story rich in passives. Past the beginner stage, however, one is more likely to be dealing with an isolated instance with, at best, an approximate recollection of the context in which one might have encountered that word or that structure before. In addition, at this stage the learner is (or should be) becoming aware of the ways in which items adjust their meaning according to context, and becoming aware also of different varieties of the foreign language. In its ability to provide rapidly multiple contexts of a particular item in an easily-scanned format, and to allow investigation of different types of text (written v. spoken, for example, or one genre or topic v. another), the concordancer is, I believe, one of the most powerful tools that we can offer the language learner, as it has been for the past quarter of a century for researchers in fields as diverse as lexicography, stylistics and descriptive syntax.

2. APPLICATIONS

While all computer concordancers from COCO (1960) onwards have many features in common, the precise facilities offered depend on the applications of the program envisaged by its designer. Since Micro-Concord is expressly designed for language learners and teachers rather than academic researchers, it might be useful to outline at this point some of the main features of the program as it is currently being rewritten (Mark II), in particular drawing attention to the extensions to the earlier version of the program (Mark I) described in Johns (1986).

1. The program is written in Zbasic (Zedcor Inc.) and can be recompiled for a variety of microcomputers including machines with the CP/M or MS-DOS operating systems and for the Apple II and Apple Macintosh, adjustments being necessary only to one or two machine-dependent routines to read the directories of data disks etc. The development machine is the Amstrad PCW, a Z80-based computer that is sold as a complete personal word processor with one or two disk drives (drive B on the PCW 8512 having a formatted capacity of 660K – in terms of text approximately 100,000 words), a RAM disk of 112K or 368K (used by the program for temporary storage of citations), and a printer.

2. Files of any length can be read, only 762 bytes of the file being held in memory at any moment in time. The program is able to handle both straight ASCII files and files prepared on line editors and simple word processors. In the latter case it attempts to deal intelligently with control characters embedded in the text, for example inserting a single space only when it encounters the sequence CR+LF for end of line, and interpreting two CR+LF's in succession as start of paragraph (in which case the end of a preceding paragraph or the start of a following paragraph are excluded from the citation).

3. It would be extremely tedious for the user to have to type in the name of every file he or she wishes to be concordanced, so the program offers three methods of selection:

Batch selection. The program examines the directory of the data disk for every file with an extension to its name that indicates it contains text that can be concordanced (currently this is the extension .CTX) and concordances all such files in sequence.

Manual selection. As above, but now the computer offers each file name in turn to the user, who has only to press the SPACE bar to accept the file, or RETURN to reject it.

Auto selection. The user is able to specify the topic(s) of files to be concordanced (e.g. Transportation and Highway Engineering), subtopic(s) (e.g. Soil Mechanics), genre(s) (e.g. Research Paper) and – for some genres possibly – subgenre(s) (e.g. Summary of Results), and the program searches for all files in the directory that meet the specification, the relevant information being coded in the 8-character file name. Many details of the classification system remain to be worked out, as it is important to find out how people want to use the system before reaching any final decisions, and the amount of information that can be coded into an 8-character name is inevitably limited.

4. The program gives a choice of three formats for examining the contexts of the target item:

Keyword-in-context (KWIC) citations with the target items aligned vertically, and a fixed width of context printed on either side. The program offers KWIC citations 74, 90, or 130 characters in width (i.e. approximately 6, 7 or 10 words on either side of the target item). The advantage of the KWIC format is that it makes it easy to scan rapidly and compare different contexts: its disadvantage is that the arbitrary truncation at either end of the citation may lose important contextual information even if the 130-character option is chosen.

Sentence containing the target item. The program may eventually offer the option of printing out also the sentence to the left and/or right of the one containing the target item.

Paragraph containing the target item, using the definition of paragraph given at 2. above.

5. The program provides for sorting of KWIC citations on one or more of the following keys:

Right Context to a depth of 1, 2 or 3 words from the target item.

Left Context to a depth of 1, 2 or 3 words from the target item. Fig. 3 shows an extract from a concordance of 'to' sorted by left context to a depth of one word.

Target item This may be required where a number of different forms of the target item are recovered by the use of a wild card: see fig. 5.

The program allows complex ordered comparisons – for example 'Give first priority to the right context to a depth of one word: where those contexts are the same, give second priority to the left context to a depth of two words: and give third priority to the target item itself'. The sorting is carried out by means of an insertion sort on the elements of an indexed 'key array' that represents in compressed form the contextual information required: this has the advantage that sorted output is available immediately all the texts are scanned, and also allows rapid re-sorting, permitting the user for example to compare the patterning of left context and right context for a particular item.

6. The user can choose to have the output shown on the screen of the computer (subject to the restriction for screen display of a width of 74 characters) or printer (with an option for more than one copy – important where the program is being used interactively with a group of students) or may be saved to a disk file.

7. The program offers three input symbols:

Wild card '*' meaning 'any number of characters' e.g.

'carr* out' (fig. 5) recovers citations for *carried out*, *carry out* and *carrying out*.

'kn*w*' recovers citations for *know*, *knows*, *known*, *knowing*, *knew* and *knowledge*.

'*ploid*' recovers for a number of related terms in Plant Biology texts: *allopolyploid*, *amphiploid*, *amphiploidy*, *aneuploid*, *diploid*, *haploid*, *hexaploid*, *octoploid*, *pentaploid*, *ploidy*, *polyploid*, *polyploidization*, *polyploidy*, *tetraploid*, *triploid*.

'in * of' recovers citations for the complex prepositions *in terms of*, *in view of*, *in excess of*, *in spite of*, *in favour of*.

Alternator '/' e.g. 'is/are/was/were/be/been/being' searches for all forms of the verb *be* in the corpus.

Context symbol '@' e.g.:

'know@+4as' identifies all instances of *know* in the context of *as* in the following four words.

'know@3as' identifies all instances of *know* in the context of *as* in the following or preceding three words.

8. One of the first things we did with concordance output was to blank out the centre column to see if students could guess the missing item from the multiple contexts. The new version provides a simple exercise generator on the lines of the one described by Rézeau (this volume) that automatically inserts a standard-length blank in place of the target item.

9. The current version of the program is designed to be used on a stand-alone basis, the learner needing only the program disk and a disk or disks of text files. It is hoped that eventually it will be available also in a multitasking version as one of the tools available to the learner from within a word processor for help in writing a particular type of text such as a technical report. In that case the learner using the word processor would be able to call for on-screen help based on:

a) Standard reference works such as the dictionary and thesaurus that can be accessed through the Turbo Lightning package (Borland International).

b) Skeleton outlines for different types of technical reports.

c) A database of texts of technical reports that the learner can access either notionally ('I'd like to look through half a dozen Introductions before writing my own.') or linguistically ('The thesaurus has suggested *hence* as a synonym for *therefore*: however, I'd like the concordancer to show me some contexts for both words before deciding which to choose.')

10. There are certain facilities that Micro-Concord does not currently offer, although they are usual on mainframe concordancers used for linguistic and literary research (Hockey 1980) and their microcomputer counterparts (Abercrombie 1984). In each case the facility was considered and rejected: in each case users and observers of the revised version have subsequently led me to reconsider what may have been mere prejudice – or programmer's laziness – on my part. It does not, for example, indicate the source or location of each citation, on the grounds that the focus of the program

is not upon the text itself, but on the language of a particular type of text as specified by the user. However, colleagues using the program have suggested that this is a feature that might well be included as it would enable the learner to examine the spread of texts within which a particular item occurs. Nor does it attempt to provide a complete concordance of all the words in a text or texts as it seemed to me that such an attempt would strain both the memory of such microcomputers as the PCW, and the attention of any student trying to make use of the printout that would be produced: however, it has been pointed out to me that a complete printout for all the texts in a particular subject area would be a useful resource for the student who does not have ready access to a computer. Finally, it continues to use the simple method of its Spectrum predecessor of grinding its way sequentially through each text file in its search for each target item, with inevitable delays where there is a large amount of text and examples are few or non-existent. Already there is at least one commercially available microcomputer concordancer (WORD-CRUNCHER from Brigham Young University) that uses the mainframe technique of pre-processing text files to produce indexed versions that allow very much faster access to target items, and David Foulds has shown (Foulds 1987) that the technique can be used effectively on the 32K, 6502-based BBC B micro.

In building a corpus of texts for use with the program we have tried to hold to the principle of authenticity of purpose, concentrating in the first place on those subject areas where we already have a close relationship with departments through team teaching and where we can call on the help of subject teachers in identifying texts that cover a representative spread of topics. Our immediate goal is to construct corpora of approximately 100,000 words for both Transportation and Highway Engineering and Plant Biology, covering a range of genres for both areas:

Lectures
Textbooks
Research papers
Dissertations & theses
Manuals (Transportation & Highway Engineering)
Technical and scientific journalism

Files vary widely in length, the longest currently being 54k, and the shortest 5k. Work has also started on a corpus of texts in the area of Business Administration, and we plan to build a corpus of examination papers in different subject areas to allow us – and our students – to investigate the linguistic features of examination questions.

3. SIX MAIN USES OF A CONCORDANCER

It is possible to distinguish six main uses of a concordancer in language teaching and learning, of which the first two could be classified as 'pre-classroom' applications: the remaining four as classroom applications proper.

The application that is closest to the academic origins of the program is as a resource for small scale on-the-ground research by the teacher in order to inform teaching decisions. My colleague Philip King, for example, is currently using the program to examine the linguistic features of report writing by overseas students, and in particular their use of nominal groups in comparison with nominal groups in target texts (King 1987), while my own interests include the use of verbs of instruction such as *discuss* and *outline* in examination questions, and features of transitivity and complementation with a small set of 'common core' verbs (e.g. *change, increase, consider, agree*) in scientific English. There is a parallel here with team teaching in the importance of the practice effect for the teacher. Team teaching requires that the language teacher keep his hand in through the challenge of new topics and new texts and the need to respond to them adequately: similarly, teachers are more likely to make effective use of a tool such as the concordancer in the classroom if they are using it on a regular basis to carry out their own investigations.

Closely linked to the first use (and possibly arising from it) is the use by the teacher of concordance output in preparing teaching materials. That use may be indirect – for example in suggesting which examples should be chosen to illustrate a language point, or in checking that the items in an exercise conform to 'normal' usage. The appearance in 1987 of the COBUILD learners' dictionary which is based on a 20-million-word corpus and which eschews the use of invented illustrative examples, and the preparation of course materials founded on the same principles (Willis and Willis, forthcoming) are now making concordance-based teaching materials available commercially for the first time, and with them the possibility of at last laying to rest some of the myths about English that language teaching has both generated and perpetuated (Sinclair and Renouf, forthcoming). A program such as Micro-Concord makes it possible for teachers to construct their own materials using the COBUILD (Collins Birmingham University International Language Database) approach.

A more radical approach is to incorporate concordance output directly in teaching materials, and to devise activities that get students to puzzle things out for themselves. Thus a sentence concordance of *if* provides an excellent starting point for a revision unit on conditionals, and shows among other things the importance in scientific English of the elliptical conditionals that the textbooks often ignore – e.g. *seldom if ever*, *little if any*. For materials on academic writing, it is possible through the careful selection of target items to recover multiple examples of a particular 'writer's move': sentence concordances of *further* (fig. 1) and *remains to be* (fig. 2), for instance, recover a number of examples of the move in which the writer indicates work that still needs to be done, and reveal both the semi-formulaic nature of such moves, and the ways in which the formulae may be adjusted and adapted to a writer's purpose.

In both the examples above concordance output is employed to investigate a fairly well-focussed syntactic or discoursal point. During the past year we have found that it can also be used for a more free-ranging and open-ended type of investigation that for lack of a better term I call 'serendipity learning'. One example of this approach is the use of massive sorted output prepared in advance of the lesson: fig. 3 shows the first page of 1,600 citations for *to* sorted by left context to a depth of one word. Working with the first page only, the teacher explores with the students the range of questions that may be asked of these sixty citations – e.g.:

a) How many of these 60 *to*'s are prepositions?

b) Which of the citations for *able to* could be rephrased using *ability to* and vice versa?

c) In which of the citations for *ability to* and *able to* is it someone that has the ability, and in which is it something that has the ability? Where the answer is unclear from the KWIC concordance, a sentence concordance (fig. 4) will usually resolve the uncertainty.

d) In what sort of scientific text does someone write (or say?) 'You're about to shove a plunger into my head' (Citation 33), and why?

e) What is X likely to be in the following sentences:
'Y happens according to X.'
'According to X, Y happens.'

– and so forth. Each pair of students is then given a different page of output with the instruction to find as many things as possible in ten minutes that are worth reporting back to the rest of the class. Staying within the left contexts starting with *A*-, this can produce observations as diverse as the likely meaning (from two contexts) of *akin to*, and the possible synonym *analogous to*: the tendency of the transitive *apply to* to be used in a physical sense ('Pressure is then applied to the roller ...') and the intransitive *apply to* to be used in an abstract sense ('... this general rule does not apply to all plants ...'): and the structure NP + as to + indirect question (e.g. 'Consideration was given as to whether ...', 'There is considerable concordance among researchers as to where ...'). There is, of course, nothing in common between such observations except for the accident that they all involve expressions with *to*. In terms of product, serendipity learning may appear trivial and its results chaotic; its value lies in the discovery processes involved and the way in which it points up the various ways in which context – even the limited context of the KWIC concordance – can be investigated.

The concordancer can also be used interactively by teacher and students during the lesson either as a focus of classroom activities, or as a 'sleeping resource' to be used to help answer questions as they arise. As an example of the first use, we have exploited the program to examine with students how terms for certain common core scientific concepts (e.g. *problem*, *experiment*, *result*) are used in text. With *experiment* our attention was first drawn to the ways in which experiments are named (e.g. '... a series of experiments carried out by Frederick L. Heffron, Craig Rubens at the University of Washington and continued by Heffron and his colleagues at the University of California at San Francisco.') and described (e.g. '... genetic experiments aimed at understanding how the Mu DNA interacts with other DNA in a bacterial cell.'). Looking at the verbs used with *experiment*, we noticed that although the textbooks on scientific English usually give to *do*, *carry out* and *perform* an experiment as equivalent alternatives, our texts only had examples of *do* (4 citations) and *carry out* (8 citations). That led to the question 'What else apart from experiments can be carried out?' – a concordance of *carr** out (fig. 5) showed *tests*, *trials*, *work*, *studies*, *programs*, *investigations* and *processes* (including named processes such as *a final heating and mixing* and *nonhomologous recombination*). We noted also that the concordance showed no example of 'carry out a report/paper/thesis etc.', which is an overgeneralisation occasionally encountered in the writing of overseas students.

The value of the concordancer as a sleeping resource is well illustrated by the question about the difference between *therefore* and *hence*. Standard works of reference having proved generally unhelpful (one recent dictionary, for example defining *therefore* as meaning 'for that reason' and *hence* as meaning 'for this reason'), we decided to turn to the concordancer, and to add *consequently* as a third connective that it might be useful to compare with the first two. From the output (fig. 6) we observed *inter alia* that

a) All three connectives are found in the texts, with *therefore* occurring more frequently than either of the other two.

b) In recent years much attention has been paid in ESP materials to connectives, *therefore* usually being presented in sentence-initial position

(Sentence 1. Therefore(,) Sentence 2.) While this does appear to be the typical use of *consequently* (6/8 citations) and an important use of *hence* (4/10 citations), it seems to be relatively infrequent with *therefore* (4/42 citations).

c) A characteristic placing of *therefore* is in pre-verb position ('It therefore appears ...', '... has therefore depended...') or after *be* ('... are therefore likely ...'). Neither *hence* nor *consequently* are found in these positions in the texts. One interpretation of this result is that *therefore* enters more readily into the flow of the argument than the other two – it is a consequence to be expected rather than one to which attention needs to be drawn.

d) All three connectives appear after *and*, the coordination being between Clauses (citations 2), 3), 5) and 7) for *therefore*, 2) and 4) for *hence*, and 1) for *consequently*), Predicates (citations 1) and 6) for *therefore*, 1) for *hence* and 2) for *consequently*), and Noun Phrases (citations 4) for *therefore*, and 2), 5) and 6) for *hence*). In the case of citations 2) and 7) for *therefore* the level of coordination is unclear from the KWIC concordance alone, and was checked against a sentence concordance. This result suggests that one typical use of *hence* is to introduce elliptical asides outside the main flow of the argument – notice, for example, the use of parentheses in citations 3) and 5).

4. CONCLUSIONS

The limited data on which the results for *therefore* and *hence* are based would, of course, rule out the above description as a piece of pure linguistic research, as would the concentration on local features of connective placement without any reference to a theory of cohesion in discourse, or any examination of the overall structure of argument in the texts – though use of the paragraph option of Micro-Concord could, of course, be used to help shed light on the latter. Nevertheless, this can serve as a fair example of the 'research on the hop' that an interactive concordancer makes possible. Firstly the results are *credible*. If I had had to answer the initial question off the top of my head I would have been unlikely to have hit upon anything like the above, except possibly for a) – and I hope I would have been wary of making even that statement on the basis of intuition alone. It is some consolation that most experienced teachers of English to whom I have posed the same question have been unable to do any better, offering generalisations that either fly in the face of the evidence or are so wonderfully vague that they could hardly be of much help to the learner. Nevertheless, it is characteristic of data-based research that the results are, in fact, completely unsurprising: as a native speaker one's reaction is 'Yes, of course, that is how I use *hence* myself'. For the teacher, the power and the beauty of the concordancer is that it shows what one knows, in a sense, already but can only with difficulty bring to consciousness: might not that at times be its value to the learner also? Secondly, the results are *usable*. When a student asks a question such as 'What is the difference between *therefore* and *hence*?', (s)he is as likely to be concerned with such mundane matters as the placement of the connectives and differences in meaning that can be associated with differences in placement as with anything else. Thirdly, the results are *attainable*: they do not require any deep training in theoretical linguistics, although an ability to recognize constituents such as Noun Phrase, Predicate and Clause will clearly be useful. Experience suggests that some basic training in 'strategies of observation' will help students get the most out of data-based learning – for example in giving them practice in identification and classification (multicoloured fibre-tip pens for marking up contexts are an excellent auxiliary tool) or in devising exercises which require them to move from observation of immediate context to observation of wider context (including practice in guessing what lies beyond the arbitrarily truncated horizon of the KWIC citation). How much training is required will depend on the students and their previous experience: my own not only pick up the general idea remarkably quickly, but show that they have done so by noticing things in the data that I have not noticed myself. And fourthly, the results are *transferable*, both in the narrow sense that the pattern of observations can be repeated with a range of other connectives (*however*, *nevertheless/nonetheless* and *on the other hand* giving some interesting results) and in the wider sense that they can help to alert learners to the importance of placement in general in English. Transfer of the strategies learned with the concordancer to the situation in which the learner is working with straight text may well take place naturally (research could usefully be done in this area) and could be encouraged by a variety of follow-up activities away from the computer.

Once students have learned how to use the program effectively, a concordancer can be made available on a self-access basis either as a stand-alone program, or, as suggested previously, as a facility available from within a word processor. There are various ways in which the teacher can help students to get the most from such a facility. In Johns (1986), for example, it is shown that it can be used as a resource in helping students to correct errors in their written work if the teacher underlines an item and places a 'C' in the margin with the meaning 'You have used this word in a context which is different from the context which would be used by a native speaker. Get a concordance of the item and from that work out how you need to rewrite the context.' In our situation, self-access implies that students should have access to the program on the variety of microcomputers in their own departments, which was one of the reasons for choosing a portable language such as Zbasic for programming Mark II.

The concordancer can be such a powerful tool in the hands of the learner that it is important that both teachers and students should be aware of its limitations. This is in part a matter of recognizing that there are certain questions that can at best be answered only partially from the data: the training needed for using the program could well include some exploration of what questions are 'concordance-ready' and which are not. Even where an answer is available, there is the danger of forgetting the limitations of the data on which it is based, a 'possible tendency' being identified as a 'definite tendency' and a 'definite tendency' being interpreted as a 'definite rule'. That an expected form does not exist in a set of texts should not be taken to mean that it cannot exist, although it should certainly lead the learner to be wary of it. Equally, the existence of a particular form should at times be treated with caution. For example, we have found in the course of team-teaching that some subject teachers are very concerned with what they consider to be 'correct usage'. It is part of the job of the ESP teacher to be sensitive to such attitudes and to that extent to warn students about the possible risk of taking the authority of the text as absolute in all cases. In our texts we find 64 examples of the word *data*, of which 21 are marked for number: 14 as plural, and 7 as singular: this gives some basis for the advice to the overseas student that although the singular usage is becoming established it is safest to use *data* as a plural. On the other hand, of the 28 citations for *due to*, 11 are predicative (e.g. '... this respiratory activity is due to associated micro-organisms...') and 17 non-predicative (e.g. 'Due to constraints of time ...'). The old shibboleth against the non-predicative use of *due to* (Fowler 1926:123) would appear, on that evidence, to be widely ignored, yet it is still worth pointing out to students writing for supervisors who may have prescriptive and conservative views on correctness.

There is still much work to do in completing the Mark II version of Micro-Concord and ensuring that it is free of bugs, and even more to do in exploring its classroom potential. Beyond Mark II it is possible to glimpse the outlines of a Mark III which would go even further in purloining for the language learner techniques that were originally developed for academic research. Some of these are fairly obvious – for example the provision of a dictionary-making and word-count facility. One particularly interesting direction is indicated by Yang Huizhong, whose research shows that it is possible to identify, with a high degree of accuracy, the technical terms (including multi-word terms) characteristic of a particular subject by comparing relative frequencies across a range of different subjects (Yang 1986). That information could of course be of direct value to a learner or a teacher: the more intriguing possibility is that it could be used also by another computer program. Up to now the text manipulation and reconstruction programs that form a mainstay of British CALL (see above) have been essentially unintelligent and arbitrary in their operation: computer Cloze, for example, rarely goes beyond the option of requiring the machine to consult a small dictionary of grammatical words (articles, prepositions, conjunctions etc.) in making decisions about deletion. The writer is currently working on a Rational Cloze program that will give the user a much wider range of options based on a medium-sized tagged dictionary and semi-parsing rules: if such a program could also have access to information on whether an item was a technical or a semi-technical term, that would provide a powerful additional option. A further Cloze option that could be offered by reference to the results of a Mark III concordancer would take into account the predictability of an item from its immediate context – c.f. the way in which left- and right-sorted output (e.g. fig. 3) 'blocks in' commonly occurring collocates. Such possibilities would represent a bringing together of apparently very different approaches, and would, I believe, help to support the reasoned eclecticism needed to push forward the frontiers of computer-assisted language learning.

NOTE

1. This paper is an extended version of a presentation at the Delft seminar and attempts to take into account discussion at that seminar and before and during the RELC seminar in Singapore on Human Resources Development (April 1987).

REFERENCES

Abercrombie, J. 1984. *Computer Programs for Literary Analysis*, University of Pennsylvania Press, Philadelphia

Dakin, J. 1973. *The Language Laboratory and Language Learning*, Longman, London

Dulay, H. and M. Burt 1978. 'Some Remarks on Creativity in Language Acquisition', in Ritchie, W. (ed.), *Second Language Acquisition Research*, Academic Press, New York

Foulds, D. 1987. 'Computers and ESP', Paper given at RELC seminar on Human Resources Development, Singapore, April 1987

Fowler, H. 1926. *Modern English Usage*, Oxford University Press, London

Higgins, J. and T. Johns. 1984. *Computers in Language Learning*, Collins, London

Hockey, S. 1980. *A Guide to Computer Applications in the Humanities*, Duckworth, London

Johns, T. 1981. 'The Uses of an Analytic Generator: The Computer as Teacher of English for Specific Purposes, in *The ESP Teacher: Role, Development and Prospects*, ELT docs 112, British Council, London

Johns, T. 1986. 'Micro-concord: A Language-Learner's Research Tool', *System* 14/2

Johns, T. and F. Davies. 1983. 'Text as a Vehicle for Information: The Classroom Teaching of Reading in ESP', *Reading in a Foreign Language* I/1

Johns, T. and A. Dudley-Evans. 1985. 'An Experiment in Team-Teaching of Overseas Postgraduate Students of Transportation and Plant Biology', in *Team-Teaching in ESP*, ELT docs 106, British Council, 1979. Reprinted in Swales, J. (ed.) *Episodes in ESP*, Pergamon Press, Oxford

Kelly, L. 1969. *25 Centuries of Language Teaching*, Newbury House, Rowley, Mass.

King, P. 1987. 'Love, Enthusiasm and the Nozzleman', Paper given at SELMOUS conference on Autonomy and Individualisation in Language Learning, Durham, March 1987

Phillips, M. 1986. *Communicative Language Learning and the Microcomputer*, British Council, London

Seliger, H. 1983. 'The Language Learner as Linguist: Of Metaphors and Realities', *Applied Linguistics* 4/3

Sinclair, J. and A. Renouf. (forthcoming). 'A Lexical Syllabus for Language Learning', in McCarthy, M. and R. Carter *Vocabulary in Language Learning*, Longman, London

Smith, F. 1975. *Comprehension and Learning*, Holt, Rinehart and Winston, New York

Willis, J. and D. Willis. (forthcoming). *The COBUILD English Course*, Collins, London

Yang, H. 1986. 'A New Technique for Identifying Scientific/Technical Terms and Describing Science Texts', *Literary and Linguistic Computing* 1/2

APPENDIX

Fig. 1. Extracts from sentence concordance of *further*.

1) Further experimental studies of interspecific hybridisation are needed to identify the wild counterpart, the actual extent of the GP2 and whether a GP3 exists.

2) It is possible that potentially-exploitable germplasm resources exist in the other species, mainly in the other subgenus Viciastratum, but this requires further exploration.

3) Further collection and study of interspecific hybridization may yet reveal additional, accessible genetic resources.

4) Obviously further more extensive studies of experimental interspecific hybridization are needed that will of necessity be preceded by more extensive collection of wild species germplasm.

5) Further crosses with wild species in the subgenus Ceratotropis may reveal further possibilities for inducing introgression into the cultigens of this subgenus.

6) Further crosses with wild species in the subgenus Ceratotropis may reveal further possibilities for inducing introgression into the cultigens of this subgenus.

7) Further studies of genetic relationships between grain legume cultigens and their wild relatives are clearly desirable, on the lines indicated by Gregory and Gregory (1979).

Fig. 2. Sentence concordance of *remains to be.*

1) There is much that remains to be done, and can be done, to further improve disease and insect resistance, enhance tolerance to environmental extremes, and increase genetic yield potential by employing conventional plant breeding methods.

2) Whether the switching mechanism responsible for phase variation operates by a molecular process similar to transposition remains to be determined, but the process clearly falls within the category of recombination events that were considered "illegitimate" a few years ago.

3) Even in bacteria much remains to be learned about the basic molecular mechanisms that accomplish the transposition of genetic elements and the associated rearrangement of DNA molecules.

4) In the case of the M1 Motorway test section, it remains to be seen how accurate the predictions are, as no measurements have been made since 1976.

5) Although I have been able to fill a few of them since my predecessor on this theme, DR R.N. SALAMAN, expounded the situation some thirty years ago, much remains to be known, and much, perhaps, will always remain a mystery.

6) This contrasts sadly with the many records that exist for early maize cultivation in Middle America, but there is no doubt that we are only at the beginning of potato excavation work, and much remains to be done.

Fig. 3. Extract from KWIC concordance of *to* sorted by left context to a depth of 1 word.

```
 1)                                        To repeat, the cultivated polyploid wheats consist
 2)  a greater yield or a superior ability to grow in places where wheat is not grown today.
 3) t morphology together with the ability to fix nitrogen symbiotically in association with R
 4)  segments of DNA that have the ability to move around among the chromosomes and the extrac
 5) ng in-service pavements is the ability to characterize the constituent materials.  Ideally
 6) c elements extend beyond their ability to join together unrelated DNA segments and move ge
 7) aboratory have shown that Mu's ability to replicate is closely associated with its ability
 8) is closely associated with its ability to be transposed; the virus has apparently evolved
 9) you see?  They didn't have the ability to add on like, a layer of asphalt and say it's a s
10) eeds, that is, plants with the ability to colonize open or disturbed habitats with bare so
11) domestication, plants lost the ability to survive as wild plants, as mutations which enabl
12) nic races that differ in their ability to attack wheat varieties.  This discovery led to t
13) h polyploidization they have been able to increase variation through infusions of alien ge
14) ds for protein quality, they were able to retain the high levels of lysine and tryptophan
15) ampbrush" stage where we might be able to see structural details of DNA being transcribed
16)       Now, this property of being able to add together chi square values suggests immediat
17) some time ago - that we should be able to develop some tests which involve the summing of
18) rable varieties than we have been able to achieve to date.  Pathogens and insects, when fa
19) .  The wild relatives may also be able to directly confer higher productivity.
20) nt experimental information to be able to predict the half-viability period in rice.
21) cal diversity.  They seemed to be able to account for the degree of diversity observed in
22)   Not only must the chromosome be able to pair homeologously with one or more wheat chromo
23) sistance transposons appear to be able to move among very different bacterial species that
24)  these two examples you should be able to appreciate that the C4 pathway and variants such
25) la.  All those components we were able to estimate those two, because we knew the surface
26) wn; we knew the releases; we were able to estimate the spills; that was an unknown; and th
27) he shape of the reservoir we were able to - have you finished with the equation now? - Ok.
28) he shape of the reservoir we were able to say that this wetted distance here - it's actual
29) quation, to say that we were only able to treat this factor, the divergence, we were only
30) tor, the divergence, we were only able to treat those very crudely.  It was possible by cl
31) s, however.  Although I have been able to fill a few of them since my predecessor on this
32) I am, piece of soil.  Now you're about to - I'm sure you'd like to do this too - you're ab
33) u'd like to do this too - you're about to shove a plunger into my head.  All right.  Now I
34)  which make the plants more acceptable to humans. Apart from the obvious feature of the lo
35)  lus polyanthus germplasm is accessible to both P.vulgaris and P.coccineus and can be consi
36)                              According to Harlan and de Wet (1971), the soybean (Glycine m
37)                              According to Clausen (1944), 3 species of Pachyrrhizus are ex
38)                   This genus according to Verdcourt and Halliday (1978) includes 9 species
39) that parameter is calculated according to this formula.  When you're doing the chi squared
40) st section may be classified according to Lambe. These correspond to 'Type C' predictions
41) np transistor is constructed according to a different plan, in which the current flow is l
42)  the optimum bitumen content according to the Marshall Test.  Both the F.F.I. and the T.R.
43)  terminals and transforms it according to a rule embodied in its internal wiring, the tran
44) put and determine the output according to the combination of input signals.  At the heart
45) he spillage should have been according to the stage discharge relationship for the gates o
46) s or series.  Estimates vary according to the authority quoted.  Wild species are very wid
47) position of the curve alters according to temperature.  This means that the value of kt is
48) before being finally buried, according to CHAVEZ BALLON (personal communication).  The pho
49) ties than we have been able to achieve to date.  Pathogens and insects, when faced with ex
50) orld. The most impressive achievements to date have been in wheat and rice. The breeding e
51) ion involves transport of the C4 acids to chloroplasts where decarboxylation occurs, conve
52) hereas selection and drift tend to act to reduce variation.  Their relative importance in
53)  insects, and in breadth of adaptation to the best normal varieties included in the yield
54)  to pests and diseases, and adaptation to different climatic conditions.  As a result, Vav
55)  has been increased through adaptation to different environmental conditions.  Hybridizati
56) ltivated varieties), which are adapted to a wide range of environments.
57) f genetic flexibility and have adapted to a great variety of environments.
58) es, with each individual virus adapted to the capabilities of its host cell.  The RNA tumo
59)        Domesticated plants are adapted to permanently man-made habitats which have been sp
60) ressures.  Wild plants must be adapted to the environment in which they grow, and plants w
```

Fig. 4. Extract from sentence concordance of *ability to.*

1) Stakman in Minnesota during 1913 to 1930 revealed that the rust organism comprises a large number of pathogenic races that differ in their ability to attack wheat varieties.

2) Most domesticated herbaceous plants and their wild relatives are ecological weeds, that is, plants with the ability to colonize open or disturbed habitats with bare soil, and which are unable to withstand a high level of competition from other plants.

3) What is clear is that during the process of domestication, plants lost the ability to survive as wild plants, as mutations which enabled man to harvest plants more easily, such as the non- brittle rachis mutation in cereals, or the loss of legume dehiscence in the pulses, arose in plant populations.

4) Accordingly there is an urgent need for the development of new varieties of wheat with either a greater yield or a superior ability to grow in places where wheat is not grown today.

5) Thus a major problem in modelling in-service pavements is the ability to characterize the constituent materials.

6) The grain legumes are mostly typical papilionate legumes and share a common distinctive floral and fruit morphology together with the ability to fix nitrogen symbiotically in association with Rhizobium species.

Fig. 5. KWIC concordance of *carr* out* sorted by target item (1st priority) and by left context to a depth of 2 words (2nd priority).

1)	ed in the evaluation. Tests were also	carried out	varying the number of blows to try and
2)	It is suggested that experiments be	carried out	after the apparatus has been modified
3)	ixes actually laid on site needs to be	carried out.	
4)	transposable elements have so far been	carried out	primarily in bacteria, there has been e
5)	ock (1954). Much of the work has been	carried out	from the point of view of storing grain
6)	study of germplasm resources has been	carried out	in the genus Arachis (Gregory et al., 1
7)	mental taxonomic studies have not been	carried out	in this genus. If Hymowitz's hypothesi
8)	mental taxonomic studies have not been	carried out	nor has much collecting activity been a
9)	experimental work on rice is now being	carried out.	
10)	edges and Jacob experiments were being	carried out	Dennis J. Kopecko and one of us (Cohen)
11)	the wheel tracking machine were being	carried out,	it was decided to investigate the effe
12)	ymes came from a series of experiments	carried out	by Frederick L Heffron, Craig Rubens an
13)	erial cell. The results of experiments	carried out	over a period of almost 10 years have d
14)	he dynamic recurrent selection program	carried out	at multilocational sites that it is pos
15)	ood or appreciated until later studies	carried out	with the much simpler bacterial systems
16)	as I say a standard penetration test,	carried out	in a very standard way. If you're tryi
17)	Test. A series of tests was therefore	carried out	using the grading used in the V.T.M. sa
18)	The experiment was	carried out	for the ten test samples.
19)	tivation and the areas in which it was	carried out.	This will be followed by an account o
20)	ed in. A final heating and mixing was	carried out	to remove any air bubbles and leave a s
21)	the 1.4 to 1.8 range, the process was	carried out	three times before the filler was compl
22)	A second trial was	carried out	using a flat, top plate. The weight of
23)	ed and on other occasions the work was	carried out	on hulled rice. There is also the diff
24)	two temperatures: the experiments were	carried out	at constant temperatures of 15 degrees
25)	The penetration tests were	carried out	in accordance with IP 49/58 given in IP
26)	The tests were	carried out	in accordance with IP 58/56 of IP Stand
27)	Dore (1955) who	carried out	his investigations using six different
28)	Work	carried out	at Stanford and by Phillip A Sharp and
29)	Work	carried out	by Powell and Lister also confirms this
30)	From work	carried out	by Freeman Fox International on site in
31)	h varying bitumen/filler ratios and to	carry out	penetration tests at various temperatures
32)	bitumen being used. It was decided to	carry out	ring and bell tests on all samples to see
33)	e C.B.R. apparatus. It was decided to	carry out	some static load penetration tests on sam
34)	g loss of viability, it is not easy to	carry out	a critical experiment. One critical exper
35)	material in water for four days before	carrying out	the CBR test.
36)	to have several different systems for	carrying out	nonhomologous recombination, just as t

Fig. 6. KWIC concordances (written text only) for *therefore*, *hence* and *consequently* sorted by left context to a depth of 1 word.

```
 1) the remains are from wild plants, and therefore represent a pre-agricultural culture or a
 2) ost chemical and enzyme reactions, and therefore the value determined in the present work
 3) ture from the normal is not great, and therefore it is possible to estimate the half-viabi
 4) he distance between these curves - and therefore sigma - increases logarithmically with de
 5) the respiration of the seed itself and therefore one might have supposed that the seed was
 6) nsit time for an injected electron and therefore increases the speed at which the transist
 7) both P.acutifolius and P.lunatus, and, therefore, both components of the primary gene pool
 8) illsborough By-pass.  It would appear, therefore, that the bituminous material at the Hill
 9) crosses between different entities are therefore likely to be major.
10) ly, if at all.  Special techniques are therefore necessary to introduce desirable genetic
11)  and moisture content (m as per cent.) therefore has the following form [log p = kv - C1m
12) tors and viability has been described; therefore it has not been possible to predict the e
13)  For the purpose of structural design, therefore, only the numbers of commercial vehicles
14)                          What is found therefore is a situation of polyploid complexes rel
15) rence in days will not be great. Fungi therefore do have a definite deleterious effect at
16) 1.  The reshuffling of bacterial genes therefore ordinarily requires the introduction into
17) hal et al., 1978).  All Asiatic grams, therefore, have both a GP1A and GP1B.  However, it
18) free from internal mycelium and it has therefore been possible to obtain seed which is pro
19) he development of microelectronics has therefore depended in large measure on the inventio
20) bstract geometrical patterns.  We have therefore no evidence from their ceramics that the
21) if anomalous) intersectional hybrids.  Therefore, no GP3A apparently exists and the indica
22) ous combinations of genetic traits, is therefore a central requirement for the successful
23) e of Oxley and Hyde's data (Fig. 5) is therefore substantiated.
24) evice as the load element, and that is therefore the choice for demanding, large-scale int
25)  particular gene being scrutinized is, therefore, limited to that issue.  Consider the hyp
26) ormation available.  The following is, therefore, best regarded as a preliminary compilati
27) at the level of polymerase activity is therefore much lower, on active sites of HeLa chrom
28) ordinary homologous recombination.  It therefore appears that recognition of homologous DN
29) perimental work on oats and barley. It therefore seems probable that these three cereals o
30)                      Weedy forms might, therefore, be expected to occur in the random matin
31) cuits incorporating the resistors must therefore be designed to tolerate considerable vari
32)  cultivation.  The Mochica people must therefore have obtained tubers by trade with highla
33) ure content to half-viability period.  Therefore for any given moisture content the relati
34) roportional to half-viability period.  Therefore, [sigma = K sigma roe] where K sigma is c
35) f genes carried by the alien segment.  Therefore many translocations involving the desired
36) tein synthesis in our specimens should therefore have a graded set of strings of polyribos
37) cted from equation 3. It is suggested, therefore, that until further information is availa
38)  potatoes.  It seems somewhat unlikely therefore that they would have practised a form of
39)                                 It was therefore decided that another method of sample pre
40) Marshall Test.  A series of tests was therefore carried out using the grading used in the
41) istent results when crushed and it was therefore decided to revert to the 75 blows on each
42) nt authors' experimental results would therefore be expected even if the conditions of sto
 1) ossed with these cultivated wheats and hence can serve as potential donors of desirable ch
 2)  reduced affinity for one another, and hence they do not pair regularly when the cells for
 3) cessful spontaneous hybridization (and hence gene flow) between the polyploids.  Hybridiza
 4) ightly bound to atoms or molecules and hence none are available to serve as carriers of el
 5)  'cost'. Nevertheless, when light (and hence ATP) is plentiful, C4 plants in the tropics e
 6) was due to the very low compaction and hence high voids produced by the hand roller method
 7) lue assumed for the bituminous layer). Hence by choosing various values for the surface la
 8) mperature gradient through the layer.  Hence the relationship derived using the former mod
 9) te for the Hillsborough test section.  Hence the passage of 0.25, 0.51, 0.78 and 1.06 mill
10) tter-to-collector current also stops.  Hence the collector current is controlled by the ba
 1) Vavilov did not visit West Africa, and consequently this was not included in his scheme.
 2) with some of those of common wheat and consequently pair readily with them. Genes on these
 3) normal gene function in a new context. Consequently, because of the amount of heterozygosi
 4) ts and tubers are rapidly decomposed.  Consequently archaeological evidence is poor, and o
 5) tirely produced from wild type forms.  Consequently there must have been considerable sele
 6) aize for monogastric animals and man.  Consequently, it was visualized that it would soon
 7) on only one occasion after overlaying. Consequently it is not known whether the growth cur
 8) en to the point when it reaches zero.  Consequently for Oxley and Hyde's results the half-
```

Lessons from the Classroom

David Hardisty

0. INTRODUCTION

This article has been entitled 'Lessons from the Classroom' with two perspectives in mind: both that of experienced teachers wishing to hear of practical experience in CALL and that of those more concerned with the theory of CALL, who wish to incorporate practical experience into their theories.

It will firstly describe the CALL facilities in the Institute in which I work. Secondly, it will explain the basic ingredients of Computer-Assisted Language Learning (CALL), contrasting it with Textbook-Assisted Language Learning (TALL). Then, a personal view of what is seen to be three stages of CALL, characterised as paper activities, use of applications software, and world activities will be expressed. Some practical examples of lesson plans from these three stages are included in an appendix.

1. CALL FACILITIES

I work as CALL Coordinator for the British Council in Portugal. We have approximately four thousand students who come for three hours a week to learn English at all levels from complete beginners to advanced literature students. We also have a complete variety of students, from general adult, to children, to ESG (English for Special Groups) classes containing dock workers, diplomats, agronomists, naval cadets, etc. CALL facilities are a special room for CALL, computers for teachers, a 'wheel-in' computer for some classrooms, a small self-access facility in the reception, and an electronic notice board, located in the main building, all of which are connected up as a BBC Econet Network. In addition, we have several computers used in some of our off-site ESG courses, e.g. CALL is part of the self-access facilities in our teaching for the Naval School, dockers, railway company, etc. These machines are stand-alone machines. We have been using these for the last three academic years and have acquired a comprehensive range of experience of the use of CALL in various modes and with various groups, who are learning English for a few hours a week throughout an academic year. I feel it is important to emphasize that different CALL activities will occur in such a situation, where one has students for a short time throughout an academic year, compared with a situation such as a private language school in the UK, where one can have students full time for a few weeks.

At the start of the use of CALL, two basic ideas were paramount: firstly, that there should be a principled approach to the use of CALL, integrating it into the general language curriculum; secondly, the technology should be made as easy to use as possible for teachers and students. The analogy of an autobank, or cash dispenser, has proved useful here – such a facility is in fact a computer terminal: users tap in a code and then receive money; in the same way, teachers or students wishing to use the computers should only have to tap in numbers for a particular piece of work they wish to use.

There have been various arguments raised as to the advantages and disadvantages of networks verses stand-alone machines [1]. Phillips (1986:29) mentions the benefits of 'the psychological sense of solidarity that arises amongst students when they know they are using a network', and contrasts this with the need for an Institution to have a Network Manager. Some of the most pedagogically useful CALL lessons in our Institute rely on the information-transfer abilities of a Local Area Network.

2. CALL AND TALL

Computer-Assisted Language Learning can be contrasted with Textbook-Assisted Language Learning (TALL); in the latter, the attention is on using the textbook in order to achieve a teaching and learning aim; no user panics through their lack of skills at typography, graphic design, or paper making. Page x of book y is looked at from the point of view of whether it is the most suitable material for a certain stage of a course. The attention is on the Language Learning rather than the textbook per se. With CALL, the attention still tends to be on the computer. Although this is understandable during a stage of computerisation of individuals or institutions, it is important to realise that this is a temporary phenomenon. The next generation of teachers will be part of a computer generation. Similarly, new users of software tend to look at students using software at a machine, whereas once one is familiar with the general principles of the hardware, and typical software, it is possible to step back and see how they can be used in a CALL lesson, planning pre-, actual and post-computer activities.

A CALL lesson involves taking various combinations of the ingredients of hardware, software, learning strategies and interaction patterns, to 'cook' a lesson, or a scheme of work. These permutations offer a rich potential for the creation of CALL material.

Software situations vary greatly from machine to machine; most general purpose machines have adequate applications software (word processors, databases, spreadsheets, graphic packages, and communications programs), and machines such as Acorn's BBC series, or the Apple II series, have a vast range of content-specific educational software, indicating their penetration, in various countries, of the educational market. It will be interesting to see how much content-specific software will be produced on MS-DOS compatible computers. It is important for software design teams to produce machine and language independent PDL (Program Design Language) versions of software using ADTs (Abstract Data Types) – Stone and Cooke (1987) provide a comprehensive treatment of this area. Hardware is constantly changing – as are related aspects such as operating systems – and it is essential that software design from the outset recognises this and that software is written to be portable, preferably from one language to another, but certainly from one computer to another.

As regards language learning, in spite of much work in the field of second language acquisition, we are still not at the point where we know enough about how language is acquired to restrictively prescribe how technology should be used. The significance of the technological revolution taking place in society is the widespread nature of the use of the microprocessors inside computers (I have elsewhere argued that teachers will better appreciate the potential of CALL if they describe the technology in terms of its processing ability – i.e. microprocessors, rather than its computational ability – computers – (Hardisty 1987)). The last thing that is being done in the real world is to prescriptively restrict applications of the technology; language laboratories in many countries fell into disuse, as they were too tied to one particular form of methodology, which limited the awareness of their potential. The lesson to be learnt is not to limit technology to one form of methodology.

In fact, at present, our use of CALL reflects the communicative methodological principles involved in our general syllabus design and lesson planning. Fundamental ideas in communicative methodology, such as information transfer and information processing, are at the heart of two central ways in which the computer is used outside the classroom, and the proposed third stage of CALL, which is outlined below, is actually exploiting the potential of the technology to do this. This use of the technology can have a servomechanistic effect on the methodology itself – dare one say it, communicative methodology plus educational technology equals communications methodology.

Interaction patterns are a central aspect of communicative methodology. Fig. 1 represents the normal set-up in a CALL lesson in our Institute.

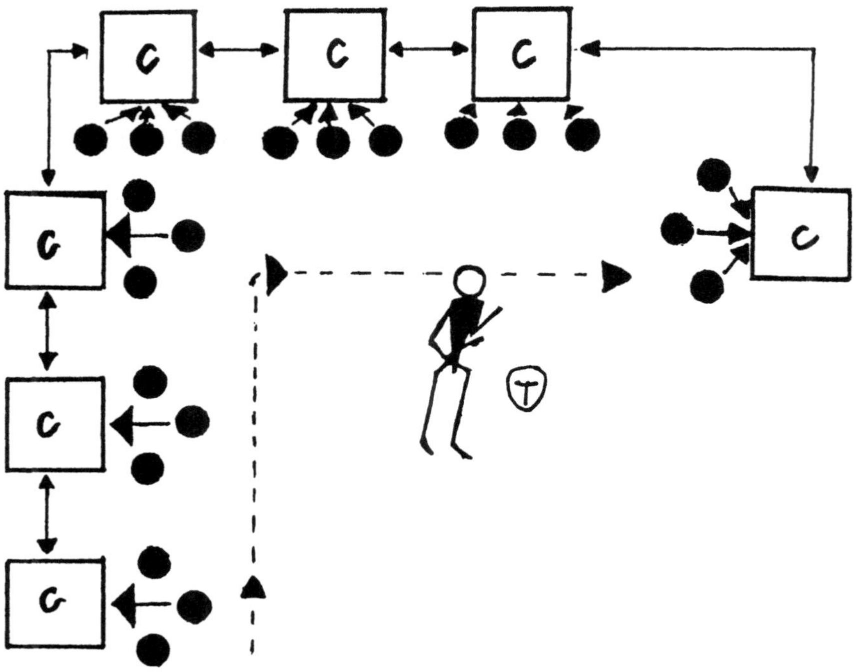

Notice the group combinations (groups of three students have been discovered to be the ideal configuration – four distances the outer two, and two may not generate interaction if a student is quiet); the arrows also indicate the communicative patterns which are possible through the use of a Network. In our Institute, we have found that such a nexus is a very rich source of information gap and information transfer activities.

A stereotyped idea is to have a computer resource for weaker students in the corner of the classroom – a technological dunce's hat, if we are not careful. Fig. 2 shows an alternative.

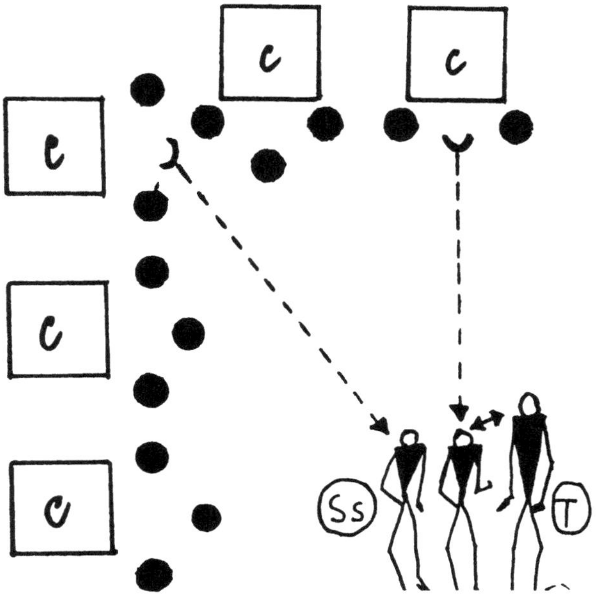

The whole class on the computer and the teacher spending time with a particular student, who has a unique learning need; this could be going through the homework of a weaker student, answering more deeply an individual's question, or students themselves choosing to approach the teacher on a one-to-one, or small group basis, to obtain the more individualised attention that is so hard for the busy teacher to provide. This is not to deny, of course, the useful role of teacher as 'roving resource' to help the computer task itself, but to emphasise that what is frequently equally exciting in a CALL lesson is the freedom the computer activity gives for what can happen away from the machines.

The interaction allows the possibility of role changes. This potential for role reversal, engendered by physical reversal (students have their backs to the teacher!) and silence on the part of the teacher until asked for assistance, is commented upon very soon by teachers new to CALL.

Any teacher training programme for CALL should include explicit components which allow teachers to realise how this reversal can be exploited. I feel it allows the classroom to become far more learning centred. This term, rather than learner-centred, has been used, as I feel the central aim of the language lesson is to enable students to learn; the optimum combination of teacher-directed and learner-directed activities depends on the individual learning circumstances, but the magisterial focus in the traditional classroom is too much on teaching rather than learning.

3.THE THREE STAGES OF CALL

In my opinion CALL can be categorised into three stages:

STAGE	FOCUS:
1. Paper-like	classroom
2. Application-like	classroom/world
3. World linking	world

3.1 Stage 1: Paper-like

This can be categorised as doing similar activities on screen as one would on paper. Phillips (1985) has pointed out that new technology tends at first to be exploited as a 'better' vehicle for older techniques.

A simple example is a program such as Gapkit (1984), whereby students have to fill in blanks. This is a familiar exercise type on paper; advantages of doing it on screen are that the computer can interact with the learners and enable them to obtain the right answer, e.g. through various help devices. Various other claims are also made for the use of CALL in this way, such as it is motivating. I would agree that the latter is true, but that one also gets students who say 'Oh dear, computers, I've spent all day in front of a screen at the faculty/office'. Other negative voices are raised – e.g. Roe's (1985) warning that old methodological wine must be forced into the bottles of the new technology (quoted in Phillips (1986)). On the other hand, we have observed in Lisbon that such software is very popular amongst students working in self-access mode, where the students themselves choose their own material.

There are two important points here, I feel. The first is that two current concerns of language teaching – discouraging slot-and-fill usage only activities, and emphasis on learner-centred activities – can actually be at odds with one another. I realise that there is a chicken and egg problem here, in that previous teaching can create exercise type expectations in the learner, but feel that the teacher and learners' common sense and experiences of learning and teaching can help them to decide what is best for their situation, rather than having it prescribed (in this sense, I would go along with Breen's (1986:51) rationale of the Process syllabus, which is a 'plan and a bank of resources specifically designed to facilitate this synthesis' (of pre-planned syllabus and learner syllabuses) 'through a decision making process undertaken by teacher and learners together.'

Secondly, it is important to recognise the important role that paper-like activities can have in computerising the teacher. If the exercise type is familar, the teacher is free to concentrate on the new technology. Once this has occurred, and a certain amount of experience has been generated, we have found that the teacher is then no longer satisfied with just this kind of activity and is ready for the second category. He or she increasingly wishes and is able to design lessons which reflect methodological principles present in general lesson design.

3.2 Stage 2: Application-like

Most general purpose Personal Computers are used for writing text, which may or may not include graphics, storing information, calculating and communicating with other computers or users of computers. Software which enables the computer to carry out these tasks is called applications software, and examples of this software are word processors, databases, spreadsheets, graphics/design packages – or increasingly, desktop publishing packages, and communications software.

Whilst this software was not originally created with educational use in mind, it is certainly possible to use it in many creative ways. Indeed, versions of the different types of applications software have been created which either simplify their use or lend themselves to educational contexts. For example, in Lisbon we use a word processsor – ABC – which was written for seven-year-olds! It is not very powerful in comparison with other word processors. However it is adequate for the majority of the lessons we wish to carry out – and, as will be seen in the example lessons, it has encouraged us to develop word processing lessons which encourage the communication possibilities of transferring information on a Network. The most important aspect of it, however, is that its use can be learned in twenty minutes, whereas a standard course to learn how to use something like WordStar would take several hours. We don't have the time. (English teachers in state secondary systems, however, may find that there is time to learn to word process – in fact, it should be one more skill that all students pick up during their scholastic years). It takes the teacher another hour, and usually some help from another teacher who already knows, to understand how to load, save and print, and transfer different texts to other machines. I am convinced that the scale of word processing that we are starting to have in the Institute would not have occurred if we had started with a more complicated word processor.

What has happened since starting to use word processing is that teachers' interests in word processing have grown. We recently offered a 'proper' word processing course – i.e. of twenty hours, either for a WordStar type word processor and/or the main BBC word processor – and half the teachers immediately put their names down for it – overbooking it by a factor of three! Other teachers have taught themselves to use a more professional word processor. Next year, more teachers will move on to using a more professional word processor with their students; the elementary one was in fact deliberately chosen, as it has a facility which allows files written on it to be altered to the form of its more powerful cousin. Thus, we see another example of the use of more powerful software being used as the degree of computerisation of the teacher increases. Word processing is also such a rich generative source of CALL activities that the teacher is only limited by imagination (see Scott Windeatt, this volume).

Databases can be rich in generating tasks which require linguistic analysis or tasks generated by problem-solving activities – some examples are given in Hardisty (1987). Rézeau (this volume) has also written about the use of databases and even spreadsheets in FRAMEWORK, a well-known package for IBM PCs and compatibles.

3.3 Stage 3: World linking

The third stage of CALL is one which I see us gradually moving towards. This involves the following:

1. Expanded use of applications packages.
2. Bringing the real world into the classroom – experientially and linguistically.
3. Enabling the students to communicate with the real world from the classroom.

3.3.1 Expanded use of applications packages

This has already been commented on above. Suffice it to say that as students and teachers become more sophisticated in their use of such software, more complicated uses of these packages become possible.

Software developers can increasingly exploit the query-language capabilities of integrated packages, and, in the long run, the similarities between such query languages and fifth-generation programming languages such as Prolog may finally break down the monopoly of BASIC as the fundamental language in personal computers.[2]

3.3.2 Bringing the real world into the classroom – experientially and linguistically

The language classroom exists, in the adult learner classroom at least, because of a perceived need in the real world. The dominant concern in language learning in recent years has been to try and bridge the gap between the classroom and the real world – witness the dichotomies of

- use/usage – Widdowson (1978),
- fluency/accuracy – Brumfit (1984), and even
- learning/acquisition – Krashen (1981).

In fact, Krashen (1985:70) states:

> 'In my view, the goal of the language class is to bring the student to the point where he or she can use the language outside the classroom in understanding and communicating with native speakers. If the student reaches this level of competence, he or she can continue to improve from the comprehensible input received "on the outside".

This type of comprehensible input 'on the outside' can be brought into the classroom in the following ways:

a. text-based corpora of written English (see Johns, this volume)

The ability of the computer to handle data, and allow the students to become computational linguists, is very powerful. It is to be hoped that a reasonably-sized corpus of written English will soon become available for all the major machines used in educational computing.

b. interactive video corpora of spoken communicative acts

Whilst extending the boundaries of CALL here, it seems to me that an excellent implementation of interactive video would be to store a corpus of spoken English; whilst the tagging of certain linguistic features would present some difficulties , this would enable very exciting searches to be carried out e.g. contrasting different exponents of a function – to find out exactly which are required in particular situations. A system such as the BBC's Domesday project offers a wealth of information about a target society, and also a rich source of information for thematic material; coupled with a corpus of spoken English, it brings the 'what' of authentic material to the classroom and leaves the learners and teachers freer to work on the 'how' – the tasks. Such a facility, I feel, allows Candlin and Breen's task-based syllabus to become far more of a reality (see Breen 1984 and Candlin 1984). It can similarly provide material for Allen's (1984) experiential component of a variable-focus approach to syllabus design.

c. teletext systems

If teaching is occurring in a country which can receive teletext transmissions, such as those given out by the British television channels, or even satellite TV channels, authentic material can be brought directly into the classroom. As an example, a reading text can be done using that day's weather forecast (preferably one that gives an international weather picture); if the same exercise is done using a weather forecast from the previous month, it is just as authentic, linguistically speaking, but has lost its topicality (its authenticity of purpose). A country like the Netherlands, which in certain regions can receive British TV, has a great advantage in this respect over many other countries.

3.4 Enabling students to communicate with the real world from the classroom

This can take several forms. The initial communication can be with the rest of the school or Institute e.g. in my Institute we have an electronic notice board; this is a viewdata system which allows us to write our own teletext-like pages, on any machine on the Network, and display them elsewhere. Students have helped to write the pages for it as well as teachers. These pages are seen by thousands of students every week. Bright and McGregor (1970) emphasised the importance of 'publishing' students' work wherever possible; the CALL extension to this is to broadcast material.

We also have network software on our computer system which allows up to nine machines to 'talk' to each other simultaneously; it can be very enjoyable communicating to colleagues who are at the other end of a building. This facility is of course very useful for practising the writing of telexes.

More ambitiously, one can link a telephone to one's computer, using a device called a modem, and start communicating with other people. Sue Hewer (1987) gives some cautionary comments about the dangers of rushing into a project, exchanging pen friend letters between schools in different countries without enough planning, but the principle remains an exciting one.[3] Short letters can be electronically mailed – one per class – and a new degree of relevance is included in the complete lesson.

4. CONCLUSION

In this article I have tried to show lessons from the classroom, in both the figurative and the literal sense. Experienced computerate use of CALL is generating and will generate further ideas for the development of both CALL, other forms of educational technology and also methodology. It is important to realise that there are ways in which CALL can be used to bring the real world into the classroom, and communicate with the real world from the classroom. Language itself and its use and skill components are changing and more channel-specific subskills are occurring.

Above all, the most important lesson from the classroom I would wish to share is that good use of CALL involves attaining a degree of computeracy where one can mix one's general professional pedagogic approach to lesson planning and syllabus design with the unique potential of this technology and produce stimulating material for all participants involved in the teaching and learning process.

NOTES

1. The British Council CALL Conference report from Barcelona (1986) and the Second British Council CALL Conference Report from Lisbon (1987).
2. See Gray (1984) for further details on logic programming and database query languages.
3. Sue Hewer, in a paper presented at the Delft CALL conference, March 1987.

REFERENCES

Allen, J. 1984. 'General Purpose Language Teaching: A Variable Focus Approach', in Brumfit, C. (ed.)

Breen, M. 1984. 'Process Syllabuses for the Language Classroom', in Brumfit, C. (ed.)

Breen, M. 1986. *Alternative Priorities and Criteria for the Design of Language Syllabuses for Adult Learners*, Department of Linguistics and Modern Language Teaching, University of Lancaster

Bright, J. and G. McGregor. 1970. *Teaching English as a Second Language*, Longman, London

British Council. 1986. Report on the First European CALL Workshop, Barcelona

British Council. 1987. Report on the Second European CALL Workshop, Lisbon

Brumfit, C. 1984. *Communicative Methodology in Language Teaching – The Roles of Fluency and Accuracy*, Cambridge University Press, Cambridge

Brumfit, C. (ed.). 1984. *General English Syllabus Design, Curriculum and Syllabus Design for the General English Classroom*, ELT Documents 118, British Council, Pergamon Press, Oxford

Candlin, C. 1984. 'Syllabus Design as a Critical Process', in Brumfit, C. (ed.)

Gray, P. 1984. *Logic, Algebra and Databases*, Ellis Horwood, Chichester

Hardisty, D. 1987. 'Personalised Information Gap Activities and CALL', *Practical English Teaching*, 7/3:35-7, Mary Glasgow Publications, London

Higgins, J. 1983. 'Can Computers Teach?', *Calico Journal*, 1/2

Krashen, S. 1981. *Second Language Acquisition and Second Language Learning*, Pergamon Press, Oxford

Krashen, S. 1985. *The Input Hypothesis: Issues and Implications*, Longman, New York

Leech, G. and C. Candlin (eds). 1986. *Computers in English Language Teaching and Research*, Longman, London

Phillips, M. 1985. 'Intelligent CALL and the QWERTY Phenomenon: A Rationale', *System*, 13/1:1-8

Phillips, M. 1986. *Communicative Language Learning and the Microcomputer*, British Council, London

Roe, P. 1985. 'Making IT Available', in Quirk, R. and H. Widdowson (eds) *English in the World. Teaching the Language and the Literatures*, Cambridge University Press, Cambridge, quoted in Phillips, M. 1986.

Stone, R. and D. Cooke. 1987. *Program Construction*, Cambridge Computer Science Texts 22, Cambridge University Press, Cambridge

Widdowson, H. 1978. *Teaching Language as Communication*, Oxford University Press, Oxford

Windeatt, S. 1986. 'Observing CALL in Action', in Leech, G. and C. Candlin (eds)

APPENDIX: LESSON PLANS

Three projects for self-access:

1. Students are allowed to use the word processor in a self-access mode in order to type in their homework. Note that this is productive self-access – the Institute only has to set up and administer such a facility, and not spend hundreds of hours developing self-access material.

2. Students can produce their own worksheets to be used in class, e.g. one class of mine this year liked to finish the week by learning the words of a pop song. Students would produce a worksheet with blanks in it (and a separate sheet of answers for the teacher!!).

3. If your institution has an English library, a book review contest could be carried out, with a prize for the best book review at each level. This stimulates writing but also reading books themselves, as a bank of reviews written by students' peers can be built up. Students wanting suggestions for a good read can use this resource (as can teachers).

Electronic notice board

If a school has software which enables teletext-like pages to be written, linked together and then broadcast, the following activities can be done:

1. The school news – various possibilities e.g. each class has responsibility for a week; or different groups responsible for different areas. For more advanced students, the news can be written in different styles, e.g. a la Guardian, or in Australian English, or very formal register, and the task is to guess the style as early in the week as possible.

2. In a class, find out favourite sports; create five or six groups (depending on size); each class writes a page which has the purpose of trying to persuade other students to take that sport up as a secondary sport; link them together; everyone reads the pages and votes on their second favourite sport.

3. Students are given information pages from which they have to extract certain information; they then create other pages which are then used by a following class to extract information; etc – student-generated material – transferred between classrooms.

The Computer across the Curriculum: English and Information Technology

Frank van Ruyssevelt

0. INTRODUCTION

Students of all subjects at the HKLS College of Higher Education in Sittard in the Netherlands have access to personal computers and are encouraged to integrate the use of information technology (IT) into their studies. Whether they are in teacher training or in general studies courses, they are introduced to applications which they can use either almost immediately or in their future careers. The main direction of work in IT may therefore be described as computer awareness; the staff of the various subject departments are responsible for alerting students to possible applications in their part of the curriculum.

1. THE DIRECTION: COMPUTER AWARENESS

1.1 Starting off with the word processor

During the first year, a general introduction of approximately forty hours is given to hands-on word processing and database skills. For students of English,the exercise material for word processing is in the target language, and consists of a number of texts about social applications of IT: networks, electronic shopping and banking, business data and government information systems. These texts have to be manipulated in various ways: activities include finding and replacing certain words, highlighting key words (boldface or underlining), glossing texts in Dutch, re-ordering the parts of a scrambled text, joining various pieces of text to form a new text, moving information from one text to another via a buffer memory, or altering text and layout to conform to the conventions of a new text type, e.g. turning a list of key words into a summary or a letter.

In the second year, the word processor is used in translation and composition courses. Over a period of time, various draft translations and compositions are marked and revised, each revision incorporating the necessary corrections and improvements with a minimum of effort – only the parts requiring modification need be worked on, and the time otherwise spent in typing out another clean copy (with the chance of making new typing errors) is saved. A clean copy can be printed out in a few minutes.

Key words and phrases noted from a text can be 'written up' into a paragraph, to be marked on its own or included into a longer text, possibly at a later date. The economical way in which the whole process of note-taking, revision, re-drafting and re-structuring a text can be carried out motivates the student to spend time on these language tasks, rather than on the mechanical job of typing or hand-copying a clean version. In this way, students are acquiring skills which will be of use to them in writing their essays in the third and fourth years of their course.

1.2 Widening the context

In order for students in the last stages of the course to broaden their repertoire beyond the basic hands-on word processing and database skills of the first years, they are encouraged in the fourth and fifth years to become aware of the symbiotic relationship that English and information technology (IT) have in society at large. They are at this stage ready to consider such topics as on-line information retrieval, the use of international databases and networks, the use of writing aids such as spelling checkers, electronic dictionaries and terminology banks, expert systems, electronic banking and shopping, electronic mail, desktop publishing and the use of English as the international language of IT in general.

1.2.1 Background information

Although several students in each group may, at some point in their careers,have taken part in a general introduction to social applications of the computer, we have found that a reader specifically related to the topics mentioned above, using texts in English, and referring, through a judicious choice of cuttings from the English-language press, to the situation in Britain, the USA and other countries is much more relevant to the uses we expect our students to become familiar with in the short and middle-term future. If communicative language teaching involves, among other things, the study of language use in situations within a socio-cultural context, then the purpose of the computer awareness input is to give the student information about the socio-cultural context within which situations occur involving the use of English and IT.

1.2.2 Demonstrations

Demonstrations involving activities in the South Limburg region of the Netherlands have proved to be enlightening. The European edition of the Wall Street Journal is printed in the nearby city of Heerlen, as part of a chain of activities involving the selection of items from the Dow Jones (owners of the WSJ) databank in New York, the editing of the European version in Brussels and the final layouting and printing in Heerlen, all made possible through telecommunications technology. Students are made aware that there is a chain of activities stretching across the Atlantic to the Netherlands, involving an important English-language medium, and making use of English language skills at each point. In the same way, we point out the use of English as the language of internal communication within international firms and organizations in the region, who use the latest electronic media.

1.2.3 Simulation

Simulation is another means of heightening awareness and practising specific skills. Since we have not, until recently, had the facilities for on-line information retrieval, we have simulated parts of the process by having students 'search' on key words through a database, and practise selective reading and summarizing on texts which had been stored in a word processor. For this process to work smoothly, it is essential to have integrated software, so that students can switch rapidly from database to text base. Although the facilities for information retrieval will shortly become available for demonstration and research purposes, simulation will remain a cheaper alternative for practising the basic skills, especially as a whole group of students can be working at the same time.

A combination of demonstration/simulation is carried out using a dedicated word processor/workstation (ETAP 4720). In one example, based on an actual case, we show how an internal newssheet is produced within a company: a selection of news, mainly in French and English, available by subscription from a news agency, is collected overnight within an electronic mailbox within the Belgian government information system (BISTEL) in Brussels; this is called up via a modem, the news items are evaluated, summarized and translated, and the relevant information is then placed within a standard layout and distributed to the desktop computers of various managers. The ETAP has an A4-sized monitor with a white surface, so that the layout of the BISTEL screen and the standardized newssheet can be seen in their entirety, complete with diacritics and accents (for the French texts). The whole process calls for a variety of language skills, including skimming, scanning, evaluation of relevance, translation, summarizing, encoding, categorizing, etc. The actual news items have, of course, not been bought from a press agency, but thoughtfully inserted by the tutor.

It is to be hoped that in the not-too-distant future, educational institutions will have access, at affordable prices, to appropriate data banks, possibly within the SURF network which will shortly link all centres of higher education in the Netherlands and, eventually, the whole of Western Europe.

Useful data banks would provide news, background facts, business, meteorological, economic and scientific data. Selections of this material could be made available to secondary schools on CD-ROM disks, and updated yearly.

The simulation of complex processes requires the use of integrated software. It is important to be able to move files from the database to the word processor, or to move quickly from one to the other. At the simplest level, we have used AppleWorks on the Apple IIe – this program integrates a word processor, database and spreadsheet, while data can be moved from the two latter components to the former via a buffer memory quaintly known as the 'clipboard'.

The program has no mail-merge facility, although this may be obtained separately. A mail-merge program can be used for more than placing addresses from a database onto a standard letter. It provides the possibility of combining variable information in texts in a great variety of ways, forcing learners to pay attention to cohesion and coherence, cf. 2.2 below. Students are making increasing use of Spellbinder, a word processor which is available to them on a Tulip System I network with hard disk. This program has a number of macro routines, such as mail-merge, selection, calculation, etc. which make it very flexible; it is also possible to build up database-like 'registers' which can be coded to permit searching. Also on the hard disk of the Tulip network are dBase II and Lotus 1-2-3, which can be used for more ambitious collections and logical search procedures. The ETAP workstation also has integrated possibilities for word processing, database, mail-merge, spreadsheeting and graphics – it is also technically possible to add communications software for use with a modem.

At the present moment, the Apple IIe computers are being superseded by MS-DOS computers, but with regard to software, our main priority will remain a flexible word processor with integrated database and spreadsheet possibilities, and perhaps communications software. Generally speaking, we shall try to obtain software which is commonly used in office automation, e.g. WordPerfect products, as our main aim remains 'real-life' applications.

2. EXAMPLES OF STUDENT ACTIVITIES

2.1 Simulation of a lexical database

A model of the way in which a single lexical database can be used to produce a variety of dictionaries has been made by two students, working on a corpus of two hundred terms from computer science. Each record contains the following fields:

English term
Dutch term
Part of speech (in English)
Part of speech (in Dutch)
English definition
Dutch definition
ISO number (for referring to the ISO terminology list)
Thematic number (a thematic ordering with key words)

The program has been constructed as an application of dBase II; the user finds himself confronted with a menu from which he can select one of the following types of dictionary:

A) a translation dictionary Dutch-English
B) a translation dictionary English-Dutch
C) a defining dictionary in English
D) a defining dictionary in Dutch
E) a thesaurus, i.e. a thematically/semantically ordered list.

If, for example, the user selects (A), he is confronted with a list of 200 words in the following layout: the Dutch term/ the part of speech in English/ the English term.

Dictionary (D) provides the following: the Dutch term/ the part of speech in Dutch/ the Dutch definition/ the ISO number/ the thematic number.

This model can be used to show first- or second-year teacher trainees the relation between various types of dictionary, and to explain how large publishing companies can produce a variety of publications from a single body of data obtained from corpus-based research (e.g. Longman's involvement with the Survey of English Usage at University College, London).

Another student is working on a similar database also including German terms – this will model the way multilingual terminology banks are used in Machine Aided Translation (MAT).

2.2 Simulation of an electronic catalogue

In order to simulate the workings of an on-line catalogue, students have made a database containing a number of books relevant to the teaching of EFL to adults. The software used is the word processor Spellbinder, which has a respectable database macro-function. The books have been catalogued according to the Universal Decimal System and subsequently categorized for the presence or absence of features such as the following:

thematic approach
communicative aims (functions, situations, etc)
communicative methodology (information gap, etc)
grammatical focus review
integrated skills
emphasis on listening
emphasis on reading
emphasis on speaking
emphasis on writing
story line throughout the book
colour illustrations
black and white illustrations
authentic material
tapes
slides
video
teacher's manual
workbook/practice book
etc.

Besides this categorization, there is a fairly detailed description of each book in a word processor file, so that the procedure can be as follows: the interested reader selects titles, searching on the above-mentioned categories with Spellbinder's selection macro, which makes a list of titles conforming to the chosen criteria. From this list, the user can move instantly to the detailed description of any title. A further possibility, going beyond what can normally be done with a catalogue, is the possibility of printing the list and/or description in a standardized circular or reading list through the mail-merge facility.

2.3 A note on simulations

Simulations such as those described above have been put onto a write-protected hard disk in a network, so that students at the introductory level can try them out without risk of wiping out the original application program. When they are thoroughly familiar with the workings of these simulations, they are able to try to make their own versions.

Although the simulations do not always optically resemble the real thing, they have the advantage of simplicity, and allow the learners to isolate the main principles involved, which is of course the main advantage of using models. In this way we are able to concentrate on the language skills involved in the analysis of data, the production of texts, the identification and labelling of text elements (discourse analysis), etc. When making their own versions, students usually work in pairs, which means a good deal of discussion during the analysis – in English, when the tutor is around ....

2.4 Essays

It is during the production of their final essays that students really come to appreciate the practicality of integrated software. The use of the word processor enables them to see the text 'grow' before their eyes – rewriting, insertion, moving paragraphs around, changing headings and altering the layout become creative tasks rather than chores. The tutor can underline, cross out and scribble comments with a total lack of inhibition, because the student is usually only too keen to produce a 'perfect' copy. The database facility is generally used to keep the booklist up to date – missing information can be filled in later, an incorrect date changed or the list arranged in alphabetical order, or in chronological order, etc. The database program can also be used to keep track of citations or notes. Spreadsheet programs can be applied to statistical/quantitative analyses. The following cases will illustrate these features.

2.4.1 English life and institutions in secondary-school course books
The teacher trainee set out to investigate the presence or absence in course books of information about English life and institutions, and the manner in which it is presented. The features on which the course books were to be analysed were the following:

1. The occurrence of information providing the socio-cultural context for situations of language use such as those described in Van Ek (1976).
2. The manner of presentation of ethnic diversity and sex roles.
3. The style of presentation of the situations, including the use of authentic texts, colour illustrations, etc.

The total list of features which the student decided to look for in the course books came to some 150 items. The following example shows just four of these; the student has taken the topic numbers and headings from Van Ek (1976:27), and listed cultural background information that she considers important for secondary-school learners:

6.1 Travel to school
In England children usually go to school on foot or by bus, rather than by bike.
6.2 Private transport

Bicycles are – compared with Holland – rather unusual. They are more or less considered as children's toys, though this goes more strongly for America. A remarkable thing about cars, however, is that there are still quite a few old cars, in good condition, on the road, e.g. a Ford Anglia or an Austin Traveller with wooden sides – many models from the fifties and sixties are still going strong.
6.5 Public transport
A typical English vehicle in public transport is the doubledecker, which is red in London and green in the country. The London taxis, and the tube, are well-known phenomena.
6.11 Traffic and traffic rules
The most important difference is, of course, the fact that the English drive on the left; they share this with about fifty other countries, mostly Commonwealth countries, but also Thailand, Japan and Indonesia. Canada is in the Commonwealth but one drives on the right. In New Zealand, Australia, South Africa (not in the Commonwealth), India, Nigeria, Jamaica, etc. one drives on the left. For foreigners this means that they should be extra careful in crossing the street – look right, not left, first! Driving on the left doesn't usually give much trouble ... etc.

This extract is sufficient to show that the list of items that the student intends to search for is a lengthy one, consisting of paragraphs of varying size. The whole list was written on a word processor, but, in this form, it was too unwieldy for use in actually counting instances in the course books. In order to facilitate the work of analysis, the numbers only of the various categories were filled in as 'labels' (which means it is not possible to perform calculations with them) on the vertical axis of a spreadsheet, while the titles of the course books to be analysed were filled in, also as labels, on the horizontal axis.

During the encoding stage, the student examined the course books and entered a 1(yes) or a 0(no) for each element per book. These numbers were entered as 'values', which means that it is possible to perform mathematical operations on them. Finally, during the analysis stage, the student was able to calculate such items of interest as:

- the total number of topics dealt with per course book
- the course books in which a given topic occurred
- the amount of 'stereotyped' information occurring in a course book
- averages
- occurrences of different presentation styles, etc.

The background theory was written up in the word processor, and the list of course books, EFL handbooks, theoretical works consulted, etc. was created in the database. The software used was AppleWorks.

2.4.2 The language of advertisements

One student within the department who had followed a course and had gained experience as an advertising copywriter decided to analyse the language of a corpus of fifty written advertisements taken from the following product groups: cars, airlines, drinks, countries/tourism and computers. Similarly to the essay described above, this analysis made use of a spreadsheet with approximately 330 criteria 'labels' on the vertical axis and the titles of fifty advertisements as labels on the horizontal axis.

The number of categories used for the analysis was actually not so large as the above suggests; the basic apparatus was quite simple, consisting of the following:

- function: six linguistic functions and five 'advertising' functions
- content: approximately 40 'themes' taken from standard advertising textbooks
- form: about a dozen formal/grammatical categories, suggested as potentially significant by Leech (1966)

Why, then, a list of 330 items? Although the matrix consisted of only 60 elements, it was applied in the first instance to the text as a whole, and then, separately, to a number of the text elements that advertising copywriters conventionally distinguish, viz.

- leading in
- heading
- subheading
- bodycopy
- caption
- panel
- balloon
- coupon
- slogan
- logotype

In this type of activity it is obviously a considerable advantage to be able to copy the list of criteria as often as necessary, creating a long list – the utility of using the computer for dealing efficiently with large amounts of data is clear to our students. When the encoding had been carried out, it was possible to calculate such items as:

- What is the average number of premodifiers in NP's in the headings of car advertisements?
- Is it true that apposition is a frequently used form of coordination in advertising copy?

- Which type of advertisement has the highest number of words per sentence in the bodycopy? (In this sample, all product groups fell within the range 12-17)
- Which type of advertisement has the greatest number of sentences? ('drinks' had an average 1.2 sentences in the bodycopy, 'cars' had 13)
- etc.

Most spreadsheet programs enable quite sophisticated calculations to be carried out, but few of our students (or staff!) have advanced very far along that road until now.

3. POSSIBLE FUTURE DEVELOPMENTS

With current budgetary restrictions and rapid technical developments it is not really possible to make detailed plans for future activities, but there is a consensus about the direction in which the department will move if and when facilities become available. These may be summed up as the PROCESS approach and the PRODUCT approach.

3.1 The process approach

Students should become aware of the whole process of the pre-analysis, selection, transformation and presentation of information – the gradient from (raw) data to information – and master the linguistic and technical skills necessary for using 'idea processors', information retrieval and desktop publishing. For this purpose we are considering the acquisition of such hardware as a laser printer, an A3 screen and modems. We are also trying to keep abreast of developments on the software front, but the situation is one of flux.

3.2 The product approach

Students should be able to analyse the most widely used text types which occur within an IT environment, e.g. manuals, descriptions, electronic mail, catalogues, thesauruses, databases, textbases, etc. and produce appropriate documents for selected groups of readers, e.g. for a wide range of ESP target groups, applying the skills acquired during the process-oriented courses.

REFERENCES:

Van Ek, J. 1976. *The Threshold Level for Modern Language Learning in Schools*, Longman, London

Leech, G. 1966. *English in Advertising*, Longman, London

The Use of Word Processors in Language Teaching[1]

Scott Windeatt

0. INTRODUCTION

There are two key features which make word processors of particular interest in language teaching: the first is the power of the editing facilities they offer the learner, and the second is the portability of the ideas they offer the teacher.

a. Power

A word processor provides powerful facilities for both creating and editing or correcting texts. Changes which would involve cutting and pasting, or rewriting, whole sections of a text written with pen and paper or a typewriter, can be made with just a few keystrokes using a word processor. Letters, words, sentences, or paragraphs – in fact, almost any length of text – can be overwritten, inserted, moved, copied or deleted anywhere in a text. The changes made can then be inspected on the screen, and alternative versions of the text considered, before a final version is decided on and committed to paper.

The significance of word processing for language teaching lies in the way in which these powerful editing facilities can encourage in learners the process of forming, testing and refining hypotheses about the target language. Learners are, on the whole, reluctant to try out alternative versions of written work, or to produce revised and corrected drafts to take account of feedback, simply because of the amount of work involved in producing these revised versions. Once the facilities offered by a word processor have been mastered, however, the economy of effort involved in editing text is likely to encourage both the initial production and later revision of written work, and in this way foster the process of forming and testing hypotheses about the language.

b. Portability

Word processing provides a partial solution not only to the difficulty which learners face in revising their work, but also to the problem which language teachers face in trying to find suitable language teaching software. Within education there has, until recently, been little standardisation of the hardware used not only in different countries, but even in different institutions within the same country, with the result that few microcomputers have a wide variety of language teaching software available for them. Word processing software is, however, available for all computers, and similar facilities are available in all word processing programs. One beneficial effect of this is that, even if the programs themselves are not portable (i.e. even if you can't use a particular word processing program on a particular computer), the ideas themselves are, so that a text, and ideas for using it, can be easily adapted for use with any computer and word processing program.

c. The exercises

The exercises described in this paper have two purposes. The first is to demonstrate the main facilities which are common to most word processing programs, and the second is to demonstrate how particular categories of language learning exercise can be implemented using a word processor. The exercises can therefore be used both as a way of teaching learners how to use word processors, and as a way of exploiting the word processing skills they have acquired, for language learning.

1. WORD PROCESSORS: THE PRINCIPAL EDITING FACILITIES

a. Deletion/insertion/overwriting

Word processing programs work on the principle that text is 'soft' while it is in the computer, and can be shaped, moulded and altered on the screen, until the user is satisfied with the result. At this point a 'hard' version of the text can be created by printing out a copy on paper.

The 'soft' version can be altered by deleting or overwriting unwanted text, or by typing in extra text. The following exercises demonstrate how these facilities work, and how they can be used for language practice.

i. 'Blind Typing'

A non-computer exercise which has proved useful in encouraging fluent writing is one in which learners are asked to spend a few minutes writing down any thoughts they have on a particular topic as quickly as they can, without worrying about mistakes in spelling or grammar. Although such an activity provides language data which could then be used for accuracy work, it is difficult to do this in practice because of the amount of correction, rewriting and re-organisation that would probably be required. With the editing facilities in a word processor, however, such revision becomes quite straightforward, and 'Blind Typing' is a simple exercise which makes use of these facilities to provide practice in both fluent and accurate writing.

Because it is so easy to make changes and corrections using a word processor, however, learners tend to focus, if anything, too much on accuracy. For that reason, the first part of the exercise is carried out 'blind'; when the learners do their initial fluent writing practice the brightness of the screen is turned down so that it is no longer possible to see the text that is being produced (alternatively, the screen can be switched off). The learners then type 'blind' for a few minutes, and when they have finished, the brightness is turned up (or the screen is turned on), so the learners can see what they have written. It is now possible to use their texts for accuracy practice, by asking them to delete or overwrite mistakes, and type in corrections (the original uncorrected text can be kept as an example of their focus on content, and the corrected version as an example of focus on form).

ii. 'Repair the text'

Some of the errors introduced into the learners' work in the 'Blind Typing' exercise will be due to a lack of familiarity with the keyboard, and one of the problems that learners face when using word processors is that until they get used to the keyboard their output will be both inaccurate and limited. This is likely to lead to feelings of frustration. There are, however, a number of useful exercises which do not require much typing, since they involve making corrections, or 'repairs', to a text that is already in the computer.

The forms which these exercises can take include:

i. extra words introduced into the text which the learner has to find and delete;
ii. misspellings which the learner has to identify and correct;
iii. grammar mistakes which the learner has to find and correct;
iv. cloze texts in which words deleted by the teacher have to be typed in by the learner;
v. errors of fact which the learner has to identify and correct by reference to other sources of information (e.g. an accompanying text on paper).

b. Block move/copy/delete

Using a word processor, text can be edited letter by letter, as described in the previous section. It is, however, equally simple to manipulate larger chunks of text, such as phrases, sentences, or paragraphs using the 'cut and paste', or 'block' move, copy or delete facilities that most word processors have. These work by placing 'markers' round a section of text, which can then be deleted, or moved or copied to anywhere in the rest of the text.

This facility can be used for 'jumbled text' exercises. The learner is faced with a text in which words, phrases, sentences or paragraphs are presented in the wrong order and in order to restore them to their correct sequence, the learner will have to 'mark' sections of the text, and move them around the screen. This operation can be repeated as often as necessary until the complete text is in what the learner thinks is the right order.

A variation on this is an exercise which presents not one, but two texts jumbled up and in the wrong order. The task for the learner is to identify which sentences belong to which text, and then to put each text in the right order. Alternatively, to simplify the task, the learner might be asked to separate out the sentences for each story, but to put just one text in order.

The advantage of using the word processor for this kind of exercise is that the learner can see the results of his choices in context, before deciding on a final version. The following example illustrates the kind of exercise for which this might be useful. The sentences make up two texts, both of which describe exactly the same process. The learner has to reconstruct the correct combination of sentences for each text by choosing a sentence from each pair to combine with a sentence from each of the other pairs. The possible combinations are distinguished from each other by reference to the discourse markers used, and using a word processor the learner can try out different combinations on the screen, in order to judge the effect of different choices.

'Rice'

Before the land is prepared for planting
When the land has been prepared for planting

the young seedlings are transplanted from the nursery, where they have been growing, to the fields.
the rice seeds are planted in a special place called a nursery.

The growing period lasts from four to six months
As soon as the land has been ploughed

the young rice plants are transplanted from the nursery to the fields.
until the rice is ripe.

The growing period follows and the plants are harvested
The harvest follows

when the cycle ends.
and the cycle ends. (from: 'Skills for Learning: Foundation', Nelson and University of Malaya Press, London ,1980)

c. Search and replace

One of the more interesting facilities that most word processors have is the 'Search and Replace' function, which allows the user to search for (and to change) particular words or phrases in a text automatically. The following exercise makes use of this as well as a number of the other editing functions described above.

'Jenny'[2]

Hi! My name's Jenny. I'm 15 years old and I live in Barnet, in North London. I'm not really sure how to describe myself. I've got a small family, just myself, my mother, my father and my dog Bonzo. I don't have many hobbies. I like skating, and I sometimes go horseriding with Ann, a very good friend of mine who lives next door.

It is carried out in 5 stages. First of all, using the facilities for deleting, inserting, and overwriting, each learner changes the information in the text so that it describes himself ('Hi! My name's Pierre. I'm 16 years old and I live in Dompierre-sur-Yon'). Then he changes all of the first person pronouns to third person pronouns automatically, using the Search and Replace function. Next, he makes the corrections which are necessary as a result of these automatic changes (e.g. capitalisation, subject/verb agreement, possessive pronouns). When this is done, using block delete facilities, he deletes any parts of the text which actually identify him. Finally the texts are all printed out and copies distributed to the learners, who then have to guess who the descriptions refer to.

This kind of exercise can be used at various different levels, as the problems introduced by automatically changing personal pronouns, for example, can include not simply concord (as in the example above), but more subtle questions of reference and style.

2. EXERCISE TYPES: PRACTICE OF LANGUAGE AND STUDY SKILLS

2.1 Making notes

Using the editing facilities described above, there are two main techniques that can be used to practise note-taking.

The first technique simply involves removing irrelevant information. Anything which does not relate to the main points of the passage can be removed from the text on the screen, leaving just the essential information to form a summary of the contents of the text.

Alternatively, rather than physically removing irrelevant information, a second technique can be used which involves marking or highlighting important points in various ways. The main points can, for example, be capitalised, underlined, or separated from the rest of the text by inserting gaps at the beginning and end of the relevant sections or, depending on the facilities available on a particular word processor, they can be highlighted by changing the background colour of a section of the text, or by changing the colour of the text itself in that section.

The following extract can be used to illustrate the process:

'Throwing Pottery'

'Well, one of the most important things in centring is the way you move – you have to keep your elbows pressed firmly against your body, otherwise you lose control of what you're doing. Now, after you've prepared the clay so that it's neither too moist nor too stiff, and so that it's well-mixed throughout, you roll it into a round ball and put it on the wheel head ready for centring (make sure that you have dipped your hands in water before you start). When you are beginning you shouldn't have a ball that's too big. It should fit comfortably between your two hands. You should turn the wheel with your foot and as it begins turning round you put your hands round the lump so that the fingers of your right hand overlap your left hand ...' (from: Cooper, J. (1979) 'Think and Link', Arnold, London)

A first stage in turning it into notes could involve deleting some of the text:

one of most important things in centring way you
move – keep elbows pressed firmly against
body, otherwise lose control of what you're doing
prepared clay so neither too moist nor too stiff
well-mixed throughout

roll into round ball
put on wheel head ready for centring
dipped hands in water before start
shouldn't have a ball that's too big fit comfortably between two hands
turn wheel with foot
as it begins turning put hands round lump so fingers of right hand overlap left hand.

The notes can then be separated out and, if necessary re-ordered, and minor re-writing carried out:

Prepare clay so neither too moist nor too stiff – well-mixed throughout.
Dip hands in water.
Roll clay into round ball – should fit comfortably between two hands.
Put ball on wheel head ready for centring.
One of most important things in centring = way you move: elbows pressed firmly against body, otherwise lose control of what you're doing.
Turn wheel with foot.
As it begins turning put hands round lump so fingers of right hand overlap left hand ...

Working in this fashion the learners can try out ideas, change their mind, and consider alternatives, before deciding on a final version (it is, incidentally, useful to have two copies of the text on the screen for many of these exercises. One is a 'working' copy, which the learners can alter in any way they wish; the other is a master copy, which is not worked on directly, but can, by using the 'block copy' function, be used to restore parts of the working copy to their original state, if the learner changes his mind about any of the changes he has made).

The final versions can then be printed out, for the learners to compare their own notes with those of others in the group (one advantage of printing is that the learners may be more willing to give and accept criticism of work presented in this way, as printing can preserve the anonymity of the writer in a way which handwriting cannot).

The notes which the learner has produced can then be revised and improved in the light of discussion with other members of the group and, as they are still in a 'soft' form in the computer, can be left in their final form as notes, with the option of using them later as the basis for further exercises.

2.2 Expanding notes

Another common study skills exercise involves the opposite process to that of making notes. Instead of taking a complete text and producing notes from it, the notes are taken as the basic data, to be expanded into a complete text. A set of notes from a text the learner has not seen could be provided, for the learner to expand into a complete text (which could then be compared with the original text from which the notes were taken). Alternatively, notes produced by the learners themselves in exercises of the kind described in 2.1 above could be used for this sort of practice. Learners could expand their own notes, or exchange notes with another learner. Practice of this kind using notes on a text which they had already seen would probably be more than simply a memory exercise, but their notes could also be used by another group of learners who had not seen the original text.

2.3 Changing a text: function and formality

Other study skills exercises provide the learner with practice in altering a text in such a way as to change the function which it performs. The student may, for example, be asked to produce rules, guidelines, or instructions using the information contained in a text. This will require parts of the text to be rewritten in order to make linguistic and stylistic changes which are needed to change the function of the text. The text on 'Throwing Pottery' in 2.1 above can be used for this type of exercise; the descriptive passage can be turned into a series of instructions on how to carry out the process, or a list of guidelines or rules.

A similar type of exercise would involve leaving the text function unchanged, but altering its level of formality. An informal description of a scientific experiment (perhaps a transcription of a spoken commentary given as the experiment is carried out) could be transformed into a formal written account.

2.4 Using a text as a model

The editing facilities of word processors also lend themselves to the exploitation of a text as a model. In exercises of this kind learners are asked to alter the content of a text, whilst preserving its overall form and function.

Such exercises might require the learner to take:

i. a passage describing a town and adapt it so as to produce a description of their own home town;

ii. an account of a scientific experiment and make the alterations necessary to transform it into a description of a similar experiment;
iii. a text describing a person's character in a sympathetic light, and make the linguistic changes which would turn it into an unsympathetic description.

The following example lends itself to such an exercise:

'In this respect both men were characteristic of the educational systems they had passed through. In America, it is not too difficult to obtain a bachelor's degree. The student is left very much to his own devices, he accumulates the necessary credits at his leisure, cheating is easy, and there is not much suspense or anxiety about the eventual outcome. He (or she) is therefore free to give full attention to the normal interests of late adolescence – sport, alcohol, entertainment and the opposite sex. It is at the postgraduate level that the pressure really begins, when the student is burnished and tempered in a series of gruelling courses and rigorous assessments until he is deemed worthy to receive the accolade of PhD ...'(from: Lodge, D. (1986) 'Changing Places', Penguin, Harmondsworth, page 15)

The book from which it is taken contains a series of comparisons, and this particular passage is followed by a parallel description of the British educational system. The exercise can therefore be used for practice using the passage as a model, and, using the differences between Lodge's description in his parallel passage and the descriptions produced by the learners, as the basis for a discussion of literary style, or of the limitations as well as the benefits of adopting models of this kind in language learning.

A learner might, for example, produce a parallel description by simply deleting and inserting certain words or phrases in the original paragraph:

In Britain, it is difficult to obtain a bachelor's degree. The student is not left to his own devices, he accumulates the necessary credits according to a fixed timetable, cheating is difficult, and the eventual outcome is uncertain and the source of anxiety ...

Whilst this is linguistically quite acceptable, it is interesting to compare it with the actual passage produced by the author:

Under the British system, competition begins and ends much earlier. Four times, under our educational rules, the human pack is shuffled and cut – at eleven-plus, sixteen-plus and twenty-plus – and happy is he who comes top of the deck on each occasion, but especially the last ...

Doing this kind of exercise on the word processor might bring home the slot-and-filler nature of the exercise (because the learner literally creates slots in someone else's text, and provides language to fill them). It might therefore serve to underline the fact that a strategy of basing language production on models is relatively straightforward (especially using the editing facilities of a word processor), but might also help to overcome the objection that such exercises tend to obscure the need for models to be presented with alternatives.

3. FOCUS ON LEARNING STRATEGIES

One of the ways in which learners can improve their skill in writing is by learning from the writing that other students produce, and by taking account of other learners' comments on their own work. This is, however, difficult, for three reasons. Firstly, writing tends to be a private and solitary occupation, because much of the work goes on inside the writer's head. Secondly, when working with pen and paper, it is time-consuming to put the words down on paper (and hard for more than one or two people to see the text as it is being written). Thirdly, it is difficult to take account of comments and criticisms of what has been written, because revision, correction and re-drafting are so time-consuming. And fourthly, students are, understandably, reluctant to lay themselves open to criticism from their contemporaries.

Word processors cannot tackle the first and last problems directly, but they can lessen the physical difficulties of manipulating text associated with the second and third of these problems, and the other problems may assume less significance as a result. The following two exercises show how word processors can be used to encourage co-operative writing.

3.1 Line-by-line stories

The first exercise involves dividing the class into groups, with one computer for each group. Each computer screen displays the first sentence of a story (the same sentence for each group). Each group has to add a sentence to that on the screen in front of them, as a continuation of the story. When they have typed a sentence, each group moves on to the next computer, and adds a sentence to those already on the screen. They continue like this until they have typed a sentence onto each computer, and have arrived back at the screen where they started. They then add the last sentence to the story. There are a number of variations that can be used with this exercise, including:

i. providing a list of vocabulary that has to be used in the story;
ii. putting a word limit on the length of the story;
iii. setting a time limit for the exercise.

3.2 Creative construction

The second example is an activity that uses writing as a preparation for reading; before beginning the study of a novel, the learners carry out an exercise in writing their own version of it. Without being told which book it is from, the learners are given a skeleton of a plot, and use it as the basis for their own stories, which are written in groups. These are written section by section, and as each section is finished, copies are printed and distributed to the other groups. Each group then reads and comments on the first draft from each of the other groups. A second draft is then prepared on the basis of these comments and subsequent discussions. This process is repeated until the end of the story is reached. Only then do the learners begin to study the novel from which the plot was taken.

The following is a skeleton plot for 'Silas Marner' which was used for such an exercise, but the activity is likely to be valuable not simply for the study of novels, but for any length of text.

1. Hero(ine) within a community.
2. Incident leads to hero(ine) being unjustly rejected by community.
3. Embittered hero(ine) leaves first community and settles on fringes of another; does not integrate, and spends many years in virtual isolation.
4. Important and unexpected incident takes place which leads hero(ine) and new community to accept each other.
5. Period of further integration of hero(ine) into community; several incidents illustrate this process, in which hero(ine) becomes progressively less embittered.
6. Second important and unexpected incident (connected with that at 4, takes place; this puts to severe test and threatens to take away his/her restored happiness.
7. Danger is overcome; integration and acceptance of hero(ine) confirmed.[3]

Reading can be seen as a process of creative construction in which the reader interacts with the text in order to create meanings rather than simply receiving them. If this view of the reading process is accepted, then creating your own version of a text before you begin to read it would appear to offer valuable preparation for interpreting somebody else's version of a text. The way in which the production of revised drafts is simplified by using word processors, and the encouragement of comment and criticism which is likely to result from this, provides a way of promoting a process of creative construction which is likely to be valuable for both writing and reading.

4. OTHER FACILITIES

There are a number of other functions which have not been considered in this paper, partly because they are not at present available on all word processors. It is, however, worth describing some of them briefly, since they will become increasingly widely available.

One of the distinctions between some of the exercises as implemented on the word processor and dedicated CALL software, is that the word processor does not provide facilities for automatically marking the work produced. There are, however, two ways in which word processors can provide at least some feedback on a learner's work. The first is through the use of spelling checkers, which can compare what the learner has written with words in the computer's dictionary. This facility is widely available but, although useful, is limited by its inability to distinguish word classes. 'There' and 'their' would, as a result, always be accepted as correct, as they are correctly spelt words, although they may be syntactically incorrect in the context in which they appear. More useful are 'advanced' (sometimes, misleadingly, called 'intelligent') spelling checkers which are able to assess the statistical likelihood of a word of a particular class occurring in a particular context, and so alert the learner to a probable error.

The second way in which teachers may be able to use word processors to provide feedback on a learner's work is by making use of the programming language which is built in to some word processing software. Using these languages, it is possible to emulate much of the CALL software currently available by writing programs which are, however, much shorter and simpler than their dedicated equivalents. This is because many of the procedures which have to be specially written for dedicated CALL software are already present in the word processing programs.

Using some of the (less-widely available) word processing facilities, it is, therefore, possible to emulate the ability of dedicated CALL software to provide feedback. Nevertheless, the main feature of word processors is likely to remain its potential for making the learner's task easier, rather than for judging the learner's performance. The availability of 'ideas' processors (a combination of database and word processor software), which can help learners to organise their ideas when writing is an example of one such development which may be of particular value for language learners. The inclusion of concordancing software in word processors, allowing learners (and teachers) to search through large quantities of text for examples of particular words and phrases is another.

5. CONCLUSION

Many of the activities described above have been adapted from pen and paper exercises, and some of them may, in fact, be more suited to this low technology medium than to high technology computers. The main purpose of this paper, however, has not been to advocate the superiority of one medium over another. It has rather been to explore a variety of ways in which word processors can be used for practising language and study skills, as a basis for assessing the benifits, if any, which this kind of software may have for language learning.

It has been suggested that the advantages which a word processor has to offer the learner are those of convenience, and the ability to see the results of proposed changes in context before making a final choice. This combination of 'soft' and 'hard' text is one which gives the learner great power to explore ideas, try out alternatives, and still produce a polished and professional-looking printed copy. Together with the 'portability' of the ideas from computer to computer which the use of a word processor allows, and the potential for further development which exists, this kind of software appears to have advantages for language teaching which are clearly worth further investigation.

NOTES

1. This article has also been published in L. Legenhausen and D. Wolff (eds) (1987). *Computer Assisted Language Learning and Innovative EFL Methodology*, Augsburger I&I-Schriften Band 38, Universität Augsburg
2. I am grateful to John Higgins for the idea of using the 'Search and Replace' function, and to David Eastment for this particular text.
3. I am grateful to Charlie Farrell for the idea for this exercise, and for the particular example quoted.

Coherence in CALL Software

Albert Sleutjes

The present situation with regard to CALL and CALL software in the Netherlands is quite unsatisfactory. There are two major reasons for this:

1. Although a relatively great number of programs are available, unfortunately they run on the 'wrong' machines. This of course has to do with the lack of standardization until recently. It seems safe to say that with the NIVO Project we also have a standard, not one that everybody will be equally happy about, but nevertheless a standard. And for any development to come off the ground that seems a prerequisite. The ungainly sight of teachers having to move machines around to be able to show a particular program will, one hopes, disappear. It was also very much a self-defeating exercise, in fact, an argument against using computers. After all machines that cause so much sweat are hardly likely to strike people as really very handy teaching tools.

2. As vital as a standard, or perhaps even more vital, is of course the software supply for the 'right' sort of machines. Here it seems that there is still a tremendous amount of work to be done. Ironically, for language teaching it is software that counts and not operating systems and machine architecture.

Of course there is quite a range of utility software like databases and word processors, but in my view, despite all the very imaginative uses one can make of this type of software, the actual acceptance of the computer in the language classroom in the majority of schools will be on the basis of good 'dedicated' software: software that is ready to be used without a lot of technicalities and without a constant demand on the teacher to be creative in finding yet another new way of using the word processor or the database. So there will be a greater demand for ready-made, applied language software than for authoring programs and 'open' utility software. In a busy teaching job teachers will look out for programs that are self-propelled.

At this moment it looks as if there might be a negative spiral: with publishers tentatively offering a very limited (and doubtful-looking) range of software for which understandably there will be little demand, which in its turn will certainly not encourage software production.

If the computer has nothing to offer to language teaching, this process is inevitable and not all unjustified either. After all the computer should not be a fashionable 'must'. At present it is a 'maybe', perhaps a 'deserving maybe'. What are the merits of the computer?

What can it do better than more traditional classroom aids? First, perhaps, a brief discussion of what it cannot do: to start with, it is unlikely to be of great importance for the oral skills; neither will it be as flexible as the teacher in reacting to the more difficult moments in the timetable, like the Monday morning and the Friday afternoon. Nor will it be an instrument for extensive reading: one does not read large quantities of text from a screen for pleasure. Moreover books and magazines have far greater portability, which is an obvious advantage.

However, the computer does seem to be able to handle intensive reading exercises and writing exercises. What does the computer add to this type of language activity?

1. First of all it adds interaction: the computer can give instant assessment of student input and by means of focussed feedback guide students through the program.

2. Moreover, this instant response will cause the feeling that the language that is produced really matters: it has an immediate effect and simulates the use of language in real life situations.

3. Students tend to feel a challenge to 'beat the machine' while working with computers. This is a harmless, productive sort of competitiveness that no one can object to.

The actual acceptance of the computer in the language curriculum will depend to a great extent on practical points of organization. One of which will no doubt be the fact that teachers will not have sufficient software to fill the computer hour for the length of a term, let alone a year. This eminently practical consideration can be more of a stumbling block than would seem at first sight. If one looks at existing software for e.g. the BBC B and Apple IIe computer in this light, one comes up against an inherent weakness in practically all of the software. A weakness that explains the feeling of dissatisfaction one feels after working with this software for a number of years: most of that software suffers from what I would like to diagnose as 'One-offitis'. With exceptions[1] they are 'one-off', isolated illustrations of CALL techniques, rather than coherent and connected pieces of software.

The adventures, cloze programs, vocabulary programs, crosswords, simulations etc.: all of these would be qualified as 'nice' or 'playful' but cannot supply the answer to the inevitable question which would then be asked: 'Is that what I do the whole year long?'

If programs are all going to be unrelated to what has been going on in the past week or weeks, then the computer hour will rapidly turn into a 'fun hour' filled with miscellaneous programs; not a very attractive thought for teachers or pupils in the long run. Moreover, CALL software, which is just a collection of loose items, will also have the disadvantage that it has to be collected: in every department one or more teachers will have to select a balanced, coherent package of software, which is a difficult, perhaps even an impossible, task for the simple reason that the available software by its nature does not 'cohere'.

This brings me to what I think are the two crucial criteria CALL programs should meet:

1. Does the program line up with the rest of the language activities? Does it fit in the course, in the topics and themes that are offered in the majority of course books, although perhaps the actual situations might differ? So does it have syllabus coherence? In other words: is it courseware?

   In this way the computer hour could offer 'practice in context' of what was taught in class, or warm up for what is going to be discussed in class later on.

2. The second criterion has to do with the internal structure of the courseware. Functional language and 'communication' do not happen out of the blue but need a solid basis in structural and lexical competence. This goes for language courseware as well: courseware should be built around a skeleton of solid components ('nuts and bolts') and therefore have internal coherence. A courseware unit might then consist of simulations round a function and within a theme, complemented by grammar and vocabulary exercises which relate to the theme and function.

Courseware which meets the above criteria can hardly be an occasional product; it takes long term planning, continuity and professional support. It also presupposes a market mechanism which keeps production 'ticking over'.

Consistent and sizeable courseware packages are most likely to be produced by commercial publishers, like the majority of other teaching materials. The NIVO Project can only act as a booster in this.

Courseware along the lines set out here would bring products to the classroom that can be planned in the syllabus. It would also stand a fair chance of being appreciated as an asset to language teaching.

NOTE

1. A program like London Adventure one can readily see used under various headings, e.g. *shopping*. Still the teacher would have to collect a package of software items, which, as I stated above, is an arduous task. This is not to say that there is no room for programs like the above; they could be used in much the same way that resource books/resource materials are used at present. However, teachers are unlikely to base their lessons on resource materials only.

Applying ALEXIS in Foreign Language Teaching: How to Develop a Feedback Database

Paul Looijmans
Carla Seifert

0. INTRODUCTION

The ALEXIS feedback program, developed by the University of Twente and Nijenrode, the Netherlands School of Business, at Breukelen, supports teachers in supplying individual and specific feedback to students. The program's main functions, technical specifications and educational applications have been discussed in a number of national and international publications (e.g. Jansen et al. 1986; Looijmans and Schrauwen 1986a, 1986b; Looijmans, Maat and Schrauwen 1987). So far, ALEXIS has been applied mainly in Dutch writing courses. It has proved to be a highly effective teacher's tool and, as a consequence, has triggered a growing interest among teachers in a variety of other disciplines. This paper is a first attempt to respond to this interest: it explores the applicability of ALEXIS in foreign language teaching.

First, we will briefly describe the program's main functions (for a more detailed description, we refer to the publications mentioned above). Then we will discuss a vital step in the process of integrating ALEXIS in FLT settings: how to set up a feedback database for a specific FLT purpose. We will propose a tentative ten-step-method for the development of such a database and report some provisional results obtained when using this method in a small Nijenrode project. The objective of this project is the development of a database for 'Wortschatzerweiterung', i.e. the expansion of the students' German vocabulary.

1. THE ALEXIS FEEDBACK PROGRAM: MAIN FUNCTIONS

ALEXIS supports teachers in one of their main tasks: giving feedback to their students. The program translates simple codes introduced by the teacher into feedback reports which tell students what is wrong and what is correct in their assignments, what should be done to improve their work, and which texts or assignments are recommended for further study.

ALEXIS consists of four subprograms:

- PROLEX enables the teacher to create feedback texts and, if desired, change or delete them.

- DISLEX takes care of printing a feedback report for each student.
- CURLEX manages student administration.

The core of ALEXIS, though, is

- SELLEX, the program for selecting feedback.

SELLEX offers the teacher a broad array of feedback texts (comments) and allows him or her to assign these texts to individual students. It is very important that teachers, just as in dyadic teacher-student interaction, can tailor their feedback to the student's needs. The teacher can choose from a great diversity of comments, depending on a variety of factors (e.g. error gravity, frequency, feedback supplied earlier, personal characteristics of the student). Such a choice is possible within SELLEX, as it enables broad and in-depth differentiation of feedback to be made. Let us review some of the options.

For a start, ALEXIS makes different *types* of comments possible, notably:

(1) Names: short texts (1 line maximum) serving as labels for the various errors and/or good points.
(2) Descriptions: longer texts, explaining what exactly is wrong or good in the assignment, and why.
(3) Corrective advice: longer texts, indicating how a particular error may be corrected.
(4) Study advice: references to specific passages in textbooks, in which the student may find more information on the errors in question.
(5) Exercise advice: references to further exercises in which attention is paid to a particular error.

Furthermore, ALEXIS allows teachers to vary the *level of abstractness* of their comments. ALEXIS feedback databases are organized in a hierarchical, tree-like fashion. For instance, a database in the domain of writing can contain a very global comment labelled 'Paragraph structure faulty' plus a variety of more specific comments with labels such as 'Topic sentence inadequate', 'No reinforcement in final sentence', 'Development of paragraph lacking', etcetera. The following example illustrates the tree-like organization of an ALEXIS database. It is an excerpt from the labels list of the Twente/Nijenrode database, from category O, which deals with topic development.

O Topic development

.

.

O11 Problem concept not adequately developed
O110 Problem concept well-developed!
O111 Problem not described in sufficient detail

O112 Why the problem is a problem not clearly indicated
O113 Inadequate description of causes
O114 Inadequate description of solutions
O1141 Solutions not in line with causes
O1142 Not all relevant solutions discussed
O1143 Solutions not discussed in sufficient detail
O1144 No evaluation of alternative solutions
O12 Action concept not adequately developed
O120 Action concept well-developed!
O121 Action not described in sufficient detail
O122 Goal not clearly indicated
.
.
.

SELLEX enables the teacher to select the desired comments from the database in an efficient way. Even with a database holding over two thousand comments (as is the case in the Twente/Nijenrode database for writing), the relevant comments can be selected in a matter of seconds.

Another function of SELLEX is the administration of the learning history of each individual student. The program keeps track of all feedback supplied to individual students, and allows the teacher to consult these data at any given moment. The quality of the feedback process can be enhanced considerably by this feature.

It should be noted that ALEXIS represents an unorthodox approach towards computer-assisted instruction (CAI). In 'classic' CAI, the student handles the keyboard and the program 'mimicks' the teacher's intelligent responses and follow-up questions. In ALEXIS, the division of labour is entirely different. For a start, it is the *teacher* who uses the program. The student receives feedback in hard copy – a report generated by ALEXIS according to the teacher's commands. But the main difference is this: whereas in classic CAI, the computer program tries hard – and often unsuccesfully – to 'look intelligent', in ALEXIS the computer does hardly more than unintelligent work such as storing, retrieving, aggregating and presenting information. All decisions – how to judge a student effort, which feedback to assign to a student – are made by the teacher. Evaluating the state-of-the-art in information technology, one has to conclude that this is the right choice. Computer programs are – at this point in time – simply not clever enough to replace teachers in anything other than very simple instructional settings.[1]

2. FEEDBACK DATABASES

As can be concluded from the above, ALEXIS is essentially an 'empty shell program'. It can only be used in combination with a database of stock comments, suited for the specific purpose in question. Teachers can obtain a suitable database in three ways: they can purchase a 'ready-made' database, adapt a current one to suit their own needs, or set up an entirely new one. At this point in time, there is one ready-made database available: the Twente/Nijenrode database for advanced writing. It is based on *Leren communiceren* ('learning how to communicate'), a communication textbook widely used in Dutch higher education. A second database, containing comments on L2 English business and technical writing, is being developed right now, and various other possibilities are being explored.

The state-of-the-art implies that in most cases the application of ALEXIS in FLT will *have to* start with the development of a *new* database. This leaves us with two questions of primary importance: what should such a database look like, and how can it be designed and built?

Building a feedback database means, essentially, organizing teachers' expertise in a certain domain into a well-ordered body of didactically effective texts. In order to achieve this, one would most likely have to make extensive use of previous efforts in the same field. When they are available, relevant textbooks and other course materials should serve as a starting-point for the construction of the database. At least, this is what experience has taught us: the development of the Twente/Nijenrode database would hardly have been feasible without the basis that *Leren communiceren* provided.

From this 'fact of experience' and from the main functions of ALEXIS, we can derive the specifications for a feedback database. First, the database should be organized in a hierarchical, tree-like fashion. Second, each 'entry' in this tree should have a label, indicating the comment in question. Third, for each entry the database should preferably contain a description, corrective advice, a study reference and an exercise reference. Fourth, both the organization of the tree and the content of the individual comments should preferably be based on up-to-date high-quality course materials. And finally, the tree as well as the comments should be based on *didactic* considerations.

Perhaps this last specification needs some explanation. It may be considered obvious, if not trivial, that the didactic nature of feedback should be emphasized. Yet, as experience has taught us, it is this very aspect which requires constant attention during the process of development. One is easily tempted to view the classification of comments as an academic task. Unlike in other classifications, however, the application of strict logical criteria is only a matter of minor concern, as the following examples will show.

During our work on the Twente/Nijenrode database, we frequently engaged in discussions concerning the organization of our 'comment tree', one of us placing error X in category A, the other definitely preferring it to be in category B. It took a while before we realized that in a *didactic* classification, such a dilemma may best be solved by placing X, in violation of 'traditional' classification rules, in *both* categories. Abandoning the 'laws of logic' may be clearly advantageous here: it allows teachers to address the same error from different perspectives. We had a similar experience when writing the actual texts of the comments and experimenting with them. Student reactions made it clear to us that didactic rather than linguistic descriptions were in order. After all, their primary function is to contribute to the students' learning process. But it is one thing to realize this and another to write about language problems without using linguistic jargon.

3. DESIGNING, BUILDING AND EVALUATING A DATABASE: A TOP-DOWN WORK SCHEME

In this section, we will explain how we started out to build a database for a specific FLT learning goal. This goal is part of the program of the Nijenrode Department of Applied Linguistics. In the construction of our database, we used a step-by-step method which could be a useful guideline for other teachers.

It should be emphasized that our method is intended to be a useful set of instructions and no more than that. Each step will have to be adapted to specific needs and specified in more detail. Other steps may have to be added.

As will be noticed, the method we propose constitutes a *top-down* approach. Constructing a feedback database does not start with writing the actual texts. Producing the actual comments, in fact, will have to be one of the last steps in the process. More often than not, working bottom-up will often necessitate ad-hoc decisions, and the resulting database is likely to reflect this. We found that an intensive planning stage is a vital step in the process of building a database.

In the next paragraphs, the various steps in our method are described briefly in the form of a set of instructions. Rather than to clarify each step in an abstract way, we have chosen to use the results of our project as an illustration.

Step #1: *Define the overall skill your database should cover.*

First, define as precisely as possible which learning goal you try to achieve with your feedback. In our project, this obvious first step resulted in the following overall objective.

Overall objective: the student can express himself in a variety of business settings by using words which are both denotationally and connotationally exact and correct (i.e. 'Wortschatzerweiterung').

Step #2: *Specify the skills that operationalize this overall skill.*

In order to do so, it may be helpful to look for 'performance indicators': aspects of student performance that you use to determine whether or not students have mastered a particular skill. For our purpose, we drew up the following list of (sub)skills:

- The student has a wide repertoire of *verbs* and selects the ones which have the right denotation and connotation in the given situation.
- Idem for *nouns.*
- Idem for *adjectives and adverbs.*
- The student uses *conjunctions* which are an exact expression of the relationship intended.
- The student *combines words* into well-formed and semantically correct phrases.

Step #3: *Develop a perspective on the desired functions of the feedback.*

Ask yourself questions like: should the feedback focus only on errors, or also on good points, or on both? Should it be product- or process-oriented? How detailed should it be? Etcetera. For our database, we came up with the answers listed below:

- The database should address *both errors and good points* in the 'upper end' of the tree (the more global comments), and focus also on errors in the 'lower end' (the more specific comments).
- As the teacher can hardly observe the students' learning process, the comments will be mainly *product-centred*; at the more global level, some tentative inferences about the learning process may be included in the comments.
- The database must allow for considerable *specificity*, to the extent that even problems with particular words and phrases can be included as separate entries, e.g. '"Müssen" und "Sollen" verwechselt' (= confusion of the verbs 'müssen' and 'sollen').

Step #4: ***Branch each skill, according to this perspective, into more specific aspects of student performance.***

Use both your textbook and your classroom experience to draw up this classification. In our case, this resulted in the following classification (only an excerpt is presented):

W-- Wortschatzerweiterung
(= vocabulary expansion)

- W1-- Wortschatzerweiterung in Bezug auf die Verben
  (= vocabulary expansion with respect to verbs)

  - W10-- Verben sehr gut gewählt!
    (= verbs well-chosen!)

  - W11-- Verb(en) zu allgemein
    (= use of verbs too general)

  - W12-- Verb falsch in diesem Kontext
    (= verb does not fit in context)

  - W13-- Interferenzfehler
    (= interference error)

    - W130-- Keine Interferenzfehler – sehr gut!
      (= no interference errors – OK!)

    - W131-- 'Müssen' und 'Sollen' verwechselt
      (= confusion of 'müssen' and 'sollen')

    - W132-- 'Sollen' und 'Werden' verwechselt
      (= confusion of 'sollen' and 'werden')

    - W133-- 'Fragen' und 'Bitten' verwechselt
      (= confusion of 'fragen' and 'bitten')

    - W134-- Hollandismus
      (= Dutchism)

      - W1341-- Verb existiert nicht auf Deutsch
        (= verb does not exist in German)

W1342-- Verb hat auf Deutsch eine andere Bedeutung
(= verb has a different meaning in German)

W1343-- Verb ist auf Deutsch reflexiv
(= verb is reflexive in German)

W1344-- Verb ist auf Deutsch anders zusammengestellt
(= verb is composed differently in German)

W14-- Umgangssprache
(= use of language too colloquial)

W2-- Wortschatzerweiterung in Bezug auf die Substantive
(= vocabulary expansion with respect to nouns)

W3-- Wortschatzerweiterung in Bezug auf die Adjektive und Adverben
(= vocabulary expansion with respect to adjectives and adverbs)

W4-- Adäquater Gebrauch der Konjunktionen
(= use of conjuctions adequate)

W5-- Richtige semantische Zuordnung
(= word combinations semantically adequate)

Step #5: *Check your classification for inconsistencies with regard to perspective (see 3), levels of abstractness, etc. Make the necessary adjustments.*

The above classification has already been examined and adapted. Omitting the positive comments turned out to be the major flaw in our early drafts. As the reader will have observed, positive comments have been included in the 'zero'-categories of our final version.

Step #6: *Determine, for every entry in your classification, which comments you would want to give to a student to whom this entry applies.*

At this stage, you will have to think about the descriptions, corrective advice, study references and exercises that you consider to be appropriate for each entry. This step should give you a first idea of the texts in your database. Postpone writing up the texts, however, and restrict yourself for the time being to key words and key phrases. First some important decisions have to be made, as will be explained in step #7.

Step #7: *Decide on a number of practical issues concerning the wording of your comments.*

You will have to decide on a number of issues here: language, length, tone, form of address, use of examples, use of linguistic terminology, literature to refer to, and so on. Remember that the didactic quality of your database will very much depend upon these decisions: in fact, at this stage you are developing the 'student interface' of the feedback. For our 'Wortschatzerweiterung' database, we decided on the following specifications.

- The comments are in German.
- They are concise, preferably not longer than 10 lines.
- The tone is advisory, assuming a tutorial attitude towards students.
- Limited use of linguistic terminology; predominant use of examples.
- Students are addressed by means of the politeness form 'Sie'.
- Study references refer in almost all cases to the textbook used, and occasionally to a standard dictionary.

Step #8. *Write the comments according to these decisions.*

When they are available, use the textbook and/or your classroom materials as a starting point. Writing the actual comments gives you the opportunity to create a 'common language': a terminology that you and your students share. Such a common language can enhance the effectiveness of the feedback considerably, so take full advantage of this opportunity: be consistent in your wording, and check it against the materials you use. Below you will find three sample comments from our database. All refer to a very specific error commented upon in the lower part of the tree.

Name and description

Confusion of 'fragen' and 'bitten'

You have used the verb 'fragen' here. This is an error which is frequently made by Dutch learners: the Dutch verb 'vragen' means both 'fragen' and 'bitten'. In this context, 'bitten' is the proper meaning, not 'fragen'.

Corrective advice

Replace 'fragen' with 'bitten' or an adequate synonym (for instance 'ersuchen'). You can always find the right solution to this problem when you bear in mind the following sentence: "Man *fragt* wenn man etwas *wissen* will, und man *bittet* wenn man etwas *haben* will."

Study advice

Please consult section 2.17 of your reader: this section tells you exactly when to use 'fragen' and when to use 'bitten'.

Step #9: *Evaluate the resulting database on the basis of your own experience with it.*

Since the proof of the pudding is in the eating, we suggest that at this stage you use the database to comment upon a number of student assignments. Find out which aspects of students' performance are not, or not adequately, covered by the database. Adjust the database according to this evaluation (this may imply going back to Step #4). As for the 'Wortschatzerweiterung' project, this evaluation has yet to take place, the writing stage still being under way.

Step #10: *Evaluate the database from the students' point of view.*

Interview students in order to get their opinion on the feedback reports your database helps to generate. Test whether they are able to improve their writing skills with the help of these reports. Find out which comments are apparently hard to interpret, and test alternatives for effectiveness.

4. DISCUSSION

It will have been noticed that what we have presented here is a very tentative outline for a database construction method. Especially the evaluation stage, Steps 9 and 10, has been presented in very general terms. Operationalizing, evaluating and refining these and other steps will be a challenge for the years ahead. Colleagues engaged in feedback database development projects, or considering doing so, are requested to contact us, so that we can share expertise and creativity.

Since the project has not yet been completed, evidence as to the effectiveness of our method is very limited. *We* find it a useful procedure, notably because sticking to it has kept us away from a number of pitfalls that we have fallen into on previous occasions. When, eventually, more database development projects are under way, our expertise in the complex matter of designing, building and evaluating feedback databases will hopefully be increased accordingly.

NOTE

1. Similar positions have been taken by the Miami group around Anandam (see Anandam 1983), who developed the Camelot program, and by Lesgold (1986).

REFERENCES

Anandam, K. 1983. 'Computer-based Feedback on Writing', Computers, Reading and Language Arts, 1/2: 30-34

Jansen, C., P. Looijmans, A. Pilot, D. Schrauwen and M. Steehouder. 1986. 'ALEXIS: Computer-assisted Feedback on Written Assignments (1)', *Computers and Composition*, 4/1: 32-45

Lesgold, A. 1986. Computers for Teaching Writing, Paper presented at the Fourth Annual Conference on Computers and Writing, Pittsburgh, May 2-4, 1986

Looijmans, P., K. Maat and D. Schrauwen. 1987. 'Een schrijfcursus via ALEXIS: Teamwork van docent en computer. Deel II', *Tijdschrift voor Taalbeheersing*, 9/2: 181-200

Looijmans, P. and D. Schrauwen. 1986a. 'Een schrijfcursus via ALEXIS: Teamwork van docent en computer. Deel I', *Tijdschrift voor Taalbeheersing*, 8/1: 24-41

Looijmans, P. and D. Schrauwen. 1986b. 'De docerende computer en andere sprookjes', *Moer*, 6: 2-8

CALL and the Integrated Professional Package FRAMEWORK

Joseph Rézeau

0. TOOLS FOR CALL

When confronted with the problems of the relative scarcity of good CALL software available on the market and of the incompatibility between the various types of micros, the language teacher who wants to integrate the computer into her teaching can opt for one of the following three directions:

a) Do one's own programming, usually in BASIC (or Pascal, Lisp, Prolog, etc.): a time-consuming and not always successful enterprise.
b) Use an authoring language, to develop 'tutorial' lessons, with the risk that 'authoring languages, with their rigid framework may stunt any teacher creativity' (Self 1985:111).
c) The third direction, which I have followed since September 1985, is that of adapting, or actually 'diverting' the so-called 'business software packages', namely word processors and databases, to suit a language teacher's needs.

1. WHY USE AN INTEGRATED PROFESSIONAL PACKAGE FOR CALL?

The 'integrated packages' usually consist of: a word processor, a database and a spreadsheet (plus a graph generator and sometimes an electronic mail utility). Best-known examples of this family are: Lotus, Symphony, FRAMEWORK, Knowledge Man, AppleWorks (on Apple machines).

Because of their powerful and user-friendly built-in facilities for word and text processing, such tools can be put to many uses, in a much easier way than programming from scratch in BASIC. The majority of the best-known types of CALL software (Storyboard, concordances, Clozemaster, mazes, automatic text generators, not to mention all types of multiple choice question tests) can be programmed using the programming facilities included in those professional tools. I have already programmed a number of such utilities, which run 'under' FRAMEWORK, with the generic name of FRAMETEACH...

One problem at the moment is that the owner's manuals to professional tools only refer to examples from the world of business and management, even though the programs can be put to many other uses (the only limit being the user's imagination).

A second handicap is that such programs will only run on the IBM PC compatible type of computers, which are totally different from and (alas) incompatible with, the home micros available in most secondary schools. For instance: the BBCs in England and the Thomsons in France. It is to be hoped that the recent dramatic fall in price of IBM-compatible machines will make such computers and the professional packages which will run on them more easily available to our institutions.

The overall philosophy behind this 'pedagogic' use of the 'professional tools' is quite in keeping with the view recently expressed by the French Minister of Education, who wants to have 'the multitude of existing small, inefficient, one-purpose, CAL programs' replaced by fewer, bigger and more powerful, all-purpose programs, similar to those used in the world of business.

The final aim is to provide the learner (and the teacher/researcher) with an Integrated Language Education System (see Leech and Candlin 1986:214). Because FRAMETEACH is based on a powerful professional tool, and the utilities have been programmed specifically for language learning/teaching, this system is both powerful and user-friendly. Because it will run on IBM-compatible computers, it can claim to be universal. Finally, the type of machine it runs on bridges the gap between the small 'home micros' with limited memory and facilities and the costly 'minis' only available to University researchers.

2. EXAMPLES OF CALL SOFTWARE UTILITIES DEVELOPED UNDER FRAMEWORK

2.0 Introduction

The central part of this article is devoted to the description of a number of programs, or 'utilities', developed with FRAMEWORK's incorporated language, FRED. These include word and text manipulation programs, mazes, concordances and automatic poetry generators. Most of those applications will be familiar to any reader interested in CALL, and I do not claim originality in this respect. I only want to stress that the use of an integrated business package for producing those programs brings the following advantages:

a) because the built-in word processing routines of the main program are available at all times, writing any of the following 'utilities' is a matter of a few lines or at most a few dozens of lines, as opposed to hundreds of lines in BASIC...;

b) because all the data that will be used by the 'utilities' themselves is entered by the user (teacher or student) as text, all the user has to know is how to use a word processor;

c) finally, once typed in, almost any text can be used for any type of activity, which has the dual advantage of being economical and pedagogically profitable in exposing the student to the same piece of information (text) through varied approaches.

2.1 Word manipulation utilities

TCH will suppress all the vowels in a given text and replace them (at the teacher's request) either with a blank, a dash or nothing at all. It is even possible to encode the text by replacing the suppressed vowels with any letters belonging to the 'international alphabet' on the IBM-compatible machines, such as Greek letters for example (figs 1a, 1b and 1c). For these and all other figures in this article see Appendix.

It is very easy, with almost any kind of word processor available on any microcomputer, to have the students do this type of exercise, by using the 'search and replace' command. This activity is very useful to make the students aware of the all-important role of the consonants in any language. You can make comparisons in this respect between the student's mother tongue and the foreign tongue, and reach the conclusion that this vowel deletion exercise is more difficult in French than English, with BIRD becoming B-RD while the French OISEAU is reduced to a mere --S---!

2.2 Text manipulation utilities

CLOZETEACH is based on Clozemaster (by Chris Jones), a now classical piece of text deletion and reconstruction CALL software. Several 'help' facilities can be offered to the student, such as looking up an alphabetical list of all deleted words (for a limited time), asking for the first letter, etc.

Apart from being used by individual students sitting at the computer, cloze texts generated by this program can be printed out and reconstructed away from the machine. If various rates of deletion have been selected by the teacher, this can lead to a useful exercise for heterogeneous classes, each individual student getting a test suited to their level.

STORYTEACH also belongs to the 'deletion/reconstruction' type of exercise, and is a descendant of the original Storyboard (by John Higgins).

Various types of help can be called for, such as guessing 'prefixes' or 'suffixes', or getting 'free' words when one is stuck. By using a built-in feature of the integrated package FRAMEWORK, it is even possible to save (onto disk) at regularly-timed intervals the actual state of the yet incomplete text, in order to study the students' strategies (figs 2a, 2b and 2c).

The use of FRAMEWORK to run both the Clozemaster and the Storyboard types of exercise brings mainly two advantages. Because you are using a sophisticated professional word processor, the entry of any text is very straightforward, and can be done by any person (secretary, teacher or even student) who has received a minimum amount of tuition in word processing. As will be explained in section 3.2 of this paper, you can even use the built-in Electronic Mail utility of FRAMEWORK to download and process texts, thus saving the trouble of typing them in.

A second advantage is that any text that has been entered and stored onto disk is from then on available for any type of activity that you choose to use under FRAMEWORK (and this means not only CLOZETEACH and STORYTEACH, but all the other types of activities mentioned below).

2.3 Mazes (and lexicons)

MAZETEACH enables the teacher to program the well-known type of CALL software known under the name of 'mazes' in only two easy steps. First, she has to type in all the location descriptions; secondly, she enters the directions into a 'movement table', and runs the program which will automatically write the branching.

Associated with the maze itself is a dictionary – or rather a lexicon of the 'difficult' words to be found in the various location descriptions. This dictionary can be either monolingual or bilingual, and it is built up by the teacher within a database. I would like to recall here an anecdote which exemplifies how a combination of professional pedagogy and amateur programming can lead to unforeseen but pedagogically interesting results. The 'dictionary' to one of my French mazes, after Raymond Queneau's well-known *Un Conte à votre Façon* (or *L'Histoire des Trois Alertes Petits Pois*), is a monolingual one, arranged in two columns: the words on the left and their definitions on the right. When I programmed the part which looks up one word in the dictionary, I intended to look up any word typed in by the student by 'searching' through the list of words (in the left column of my database). But I got that part wrong, with the result that the program searches the whole database (including the definitions) for the word being looked for. I turned this programming mistake into the following hint to the student: whenever you look up some unknown word, rather than typing the word itself, try to think of a word which might define it, type this word in, and check your guess. In the particular example I am referring to, the 'difficult' word is *ers* (a plant of the pea family). If the student types in *légume*, she will indeed access the dictionary definition of *ers*, which reads:

ers = sorte de légume, de la famille des pois ou lentilles

(Because the word *légume* is part of the definition of *ers*). This is not all: because the search for a word through the dictionary database is done using the built-in search command of FRAMEWORK, it is possible to go on searching for other occurrences of a particular word (or character string, such as part of word: prefix, suffix, etc.). If for example we initiated a search for the word *légume*, we would first of all find the definition for the word *ers*. Then, we would come to the second *légume* listed in our dictionary, namely *pois*, again because the word *légume* is part of its definition, which reads:

pois = sorte de légume, de la famille des papilionacées

We can thus use the search command of FRAMEWORK to look through a database dictionary for instances of words belonging to the same category! This is typically the sort of activity which would NOT be possible without the power of the computer. Again, I would like to stress here that my purpose is not that of linguistic research per se, but of its application to teaching and learning the language in the classroom. An immediate application of the facility mentioned above would be a lesson on how dictionaries are made (preferably monolingual dictionaries), and to actually build a 'lexicon' for use with a given text or set of texts. Let me give one more example of how an electronic lexicon built with a CALL purpose in mind can help the learner.

In that same text by Raymond Queneau there occurs the word *opopoïe*, an onomatopoeia invented by the author. When the student asks for a definition of that word, she gets the following:

Opopoïe = onomatopée inventée par Raymond Queneau

It is a common problem with dictionaries that they will sometimes define a word by using other words which in their turn are not known to the user! The word *onomatopée* would be such an example in the above definition. The way my 'electronic lexicon' works brought a solution to this problem. I entered the word *onomatopée* with the following definition:

onomatopée = mot imitant par des sons ce qu'il représente, exemples: *coucou*, *boum*, *opopoïe*

Now, because I entered the word *opopoïe* as an example in the definition for *onomatopée*, when the student asks for the definition of *opopoïe* in the first place, she gets the definition for that word first. But, since the word *opopoïe* occurs again within the definition of *onomatopée*, when the search operation continues within the lexicon, the user is automatically presented with the next occurrence of *opopoïe*, namely the definition of *onomatopée*!

To come back to the maze itself: MAZETEACH offers the possibility of printing the story as you go along through the maze, or after you have completed it.

2.4 Concordances

Although concordance programs have often been quoted in the literature of CALL, their use has mostly been restricted to linguistic research. The CONCORDTEACH utility which I have developed under FRAMEWORK is meant to help the teacher make the student aware of 'the company that words keep' (after Tim Johns' phrase), and can lead to all sorts of research and practice activities in the language classroom.

An integrated professional package allows us to produce any sort of printed output (see figs 3 to 5). This is particularly useful if you are interested in printing out whole sentences (fig. 4b). Or you can choose to put the right context of a word in alphabetical order (fig. 5b).

The following are some examples of the use of concordances in the classroom:

- analyze and give the grammatical category of a given word or part of word in its various occurrences: the French word *de*(fig. 3a) or the *-y* endings in Roald Dahl's *The Twits* (fig. 4a);
- rearrange in the right order one of the contexts (fig. 3b);
- find the missing word (fig. 3c);
- find the various missing verbs all ending in *-ait* (fig. 3d).

Finally, I have made attempts at using CONCORDTEACH to teach translation, or rather – with my pre-intermediate pupils – to draw their attention to the different uses of certain parts of speech in the source and target languages. This is achieved in the following steps. First enter a number of sentences from the source text, all numbered. In this case, sentences from Roald Dahl's *The Umbrella Man*, numbered 01A, 02A, 03A, etc. Then enter the translation into the target language, in this case French, the sentences being numbered 01F, 02F, etc. Fig. 5a shows the concordances for the English indefinite article *a* and the French equivalents *un* and *une*'. (There were no occurrences of the form *an* in the source text).

Fig. 5b shows the concordance to *a* with the right context in alphabetical order. Fig. 6a shows the correlation between the uses of the indefinite article in English and in French throughout this short text. Finally, fig. 6b lists the three instances of the text where the English article *a* is not rendered by *un* or *une*.

2.5 Automatic text generation utilities

One of the main assets of the integrated package FRAMEWORK is the ease with which data can be entered, stored, and eventually retrieved from a database and output as a piece of processed text. This feature has led to two families of utilities, both more or less based on the 'mailing' facility included in the original package.

DESCTEACH works on the principle of the 'mailing' facility, which all major database professional packages come with. The idea is that the user can fill in the 'fields' she has pre-defined in a 'letter' by using data previously entered in a database. A number of texts can thus be generated, and distributed among the students, to be used for language practice activities.

For example, 'automatic' descriptions of monsters can be generated in an extremely easy and user-friendly way (after an idea in Higgins and Johns 1984:82).

Figs 7a and 7b show how the data entered in answer to a 'likes/dislikes' questionnaire was used to generate individual descriptions from which all markers were removed. The papers were then distributed among the pupils, and this led to a 'gap-filling' activity. The pupils milled around the room, and asked their classmates 'Do you like tea?' 'Do you like black coffee?' 'Can you swim?' etc. until they got an answer contradicting the information on their slip of paper. They then went to question another pupil, and so on, until they finally found someone who agreed with all the information on the paper, and checked with the teacher that this person was the original owner of that particular paper.

It should be stressed that all those activities which result in the production of a printed text have an important impact on the pupils on the one hand, and lead to various classroom activities on the other hand, which make them well worth the time spent entering and processing data on the computer.

POETEACH: this utility works along the same principles as the DESCTEACH utility described above. But the emphasis here is not on personal data entered by the students. A number of 'automatic poetry generators' have been developed on the computer (cf Edmonson 1987). The advantage of POETEACH is that all the elements of the program: the database of words, the 'mask' (see fig. 8a) are available to the user, and can be manipulated at any time. Two examples of automatically generated poetry are found in the appendix: one in French, based on Baudelaire's *L'Invitation au Voyage* (figs 8a to 8c), and one in English, based on a song from an English textbook in use in French schools (fig. 9).

The pedagogic interest of such automatically generated texts or poems rests not so much with the texts themselves as with a) the preparatory work which leads to the automatic generation, and b) the exploitation of the texts.

The teacher's first task consists in drawing the students' attention to the structure of the text or poem which is to serve as the model, or 'frame' for the automatic generation operation. Even with beginners or pre-intermediate pupils, this is worthwhile and not too difficult. A discussion about which parts of the text will be kept to make the 'frame' and which parts will be deleted in order to be replaced later on at random with words or phrases of the same categories makes the students aware of how language works.

Papert (1980:48) cites the example of a young girl who after working with that sort of program said 'Now I know why we have nouns and verbs!'. When I had told my own pupils that we needed a number of adjectives to fill in a particular column of the database used to make the 'Computer Rainbow' poem, a number of enthusiastic pupils came to the following lesson with long lists. It is doubtful that a similar request for lists of adjectives set for homework without the motivation of contributing to the automatic generation of a poem would have met with such results.

Here follows an account of how the automatically generated poems 'River Rainbow' were used in class. I printed as many different poems as there are pupils in the class, and gave a poem to each of them (fig. 9). This generated a lot of excitement, as the pupils read through the rather surrealistic lines and then went to their neighbours to see what they'd got. Then I asked them to work in pairs and between the two of them to make out one poem out of the two they'd got, by selecting the lines they liked most or which made most sense to them. Then they worked in fours, and again made up one poem out of the two which came from the two pairs, then in eights. Finally, the two or three 'best poems' were written on the blackboard and copied in the students' copybooks. For the following week, the pupils were invited to illustrate their favourite poems, or just stanzas or even lines, and the drawings or collages were pinned to the classroom walls, together with the lines they illustrated.

I have chosen to write at length about this particular activity because it is my favourite example of how the computer can be used to stimulate creativity with the students (and the teacher!).

3. FUTURE DEVELOPMENTS

3.1 Dictionaries and spelling checkers

FRAMEWORK comes with an integrated dictionary, or rather a 'spelling checker'. This is mainly meant as an aid to check typing mistakes or spelling mistakes, but it will accept any word that is present in its word database, regardless of its impropriety of use. Unfortunately, the American version of FRAMEWORK comes with an English dictionary, and the French version comes with a French dictionary, but these two dictionaries are not (yet?) available at the same time from within a given version of the package. A facility which would allow immediate access to bilingual dictionaries would be a boon to CALL users.

In the meantime, it is still possible to build up your own 'personal dictionaries'. It is even possible to turn the contents of any given text into a dictionary. This means that even if you are using, say the French version of FRAMEWORK, you can build up a personal dictionary in any other language. This facility could be used for example as a spelling checker in a dictation activity. The teacher types in a text and asks FRAMEWORK to turn this text into a dictionary. Then the teacher (or a recording) dictates the text, which the student types in (under FRAMEWORK). When the student has finished writing, she can call up the 'personal dictionary' containing all the words of the text, and this will automatically check her mistakes, and indeed 'suggest' corrections!

3.2 Electronic mail, teletext, etc.

FRAMEWORK comes with a built-in electronic communications facility. This means that, provided you connect your computer to a modem, you can – via the telephone – plug into any databank of the 'teletext' type and download texts into your machine, and process them later on at your leisure. For example, at the moment in France, it is possible to download whole pages of news in English by dialling 36-15 (for one of our Teletext centers) and typing on your computer the code 'BBC'!

This means that from within FRAMEWORK you can gather huge quantities of text without having to type it in. Then you can use any of the FRAMETEACH utilities to process those texts in any way you wish. The time is not far when it will be possible to switch on your computer when you get up in the morning, hook on to the BBC teletext news service, download one or two pages of fresh news, call up the CLOZETEACH utility under FRAMETEACH, and take a printout of the morning's news in cloze form, ready to be photocopied and handed out to your students ... all of this while you are having your breakfast!

REFERENCES

Edmonson, W. 1987. ' "Meaningful Input" and Meaningful Learning: A Poetry Generator', in Legenhausen, L. and D. Wolff (eds) *Computer Assisted Language Learning and Innovative EFL Methodology*, Augsburger I & I-Schriften Band 38, Universität Augsburg

Higgins, J. and T. Johns. 1984. *Computers in Language Learning*, Collins, London

Leech, G. and C. Candlin (eds). 1986. *Computers in English Language Teaching and Research*, Longman, London

Papert, S. 1980. *Mindstorms: Children, Computers and Powerful Ideas*, Basic Books, New York

Self, J. 1985. *Microcomputers in Education*, Harvester Press, Brighton

APPENDIX

Figure 1a.

Mr Tw-t w-s -n- -f th-s- v-ry h--ry-f-c-d m-n. Th- wh-l- -f h-s f-c- -xc-pt f-r h-s f-r-h--d, h-s -y-s -nd h-s n-s- w-s c-v-r-d w-th th-ck h--r. Mr Tw-t f-lt th-t h-s h--r-n-ss m-d- h-m l--k w-s- -nd gr-nd. B-t -n tr-th h- w-s n--th-r -f th-s- th-ngs. Mr Tw-t w-s - tw-t. H- w-s b-rn - tw-t. -nd n-w, -t th- -g- -f s-xty, h- w-s - b-gg-r tw-t th-n -v-r. Th- h--r -n Mr Tw-t's f-c- gr-w -n sp-k-s th-t st-ck --t str--ght l-k- th- br-stl-s -f - h--rbr-sh. -nd h-w -ft-n d-d Mr Tw-t w-sh th-s br-stly, n--l-br-shy f-c- -f h-s? Th- -nsw-r -s N-V-R, n-t -v-n -n S-nd-ys. H- h-dn't w-sh-d -t f-r y--rs.

Figure 1b.

Mr Twt ws n f ths vry hryfcd mn. Th whl f hs fc xcpt fr hs frhd, hs ys nd hs ns ws cvrd wth thck hr. Mr Twt flt tht hs hrnss md hm lk ws nd grnd. Bt n trth h ws nthr f ths thngs. Mr Twt ws twt. H ws brn twt. nd nw, t th g f sxty, h ws bggr twt thn vr. Th hr n Mr Twt's fc grw n spks tht stck t strght lk th brstls f hrbrsh. nd hw ftn dd Mr Twt wsh ths brstly, nlbrshy fc f hs? Th nswr s NVR, nt vn n Sndys. H hdn't wshd t fr yrs.

Figure 1c.

Mr Tw∩t w≡s θnϕ θf thϕsϕ vϕr⊥ h≡∩r⊥-f≡cϕd mϕn. Thϕ whθlϕ θf h∩s f≡cϕ ϕxcϕpt fθr h∩s fθrϕhϕ≡d, h∩s ϕ⊥ϕs ≡nd h∩s nθsϕ w≡s cθvϕrϕd w∩th th∩ck h≡∩r. Mr Tw∩t fϕlt th≡t h∩s h≡∩r∩nϕss m≡dϕ h∩m lθθk w∩sϕ ≡nd gr≡nd. Bψt ∩n trψth hϕ w≡s nϕ∩thϕr θf thϕsϕ th∩ngs. Mr Tw∩t w≡s ≡ tw∩t. Hϕ w≡s bθrn ≡ tw∩t. ≡nd nθw, ≡t thϕ ≡gϕ θf s∩xt⊥, hϕ w≡s ≡ b∩ggϕr tw∩t th≡n ϕvϕr. Thϕ h≡∩r θn Mr Tw∩t's f≡cϕ grϕw ∩n sp∩kϕs th≡t stψck θψt str≡∩ght l∩kϕ thϕ br∩stlϕs θf ≡ h≡∩rbrψsh. ≡nd hθw θftϕn d∩d Mr Tw∩t w≡sh th∩s br∩stl⊥, n≡∩l-brψsh⊥ f≡cϕ θf h∩s? Thϕ ≡nswϕr ∩s NϕVϕR, nθt ϕvϕn θn Sψnd≡⊥s. Hϕ h≡dn't w≡shϕd ∩t fθr ⊥ϕ≡rs.

Figure 2a.

Mr Twit was one of these very hairy-faced men. The whole of his face except for his forehead, his eyes and his nose was covered with thick hair. Mr Twit felt that his hairiness made him look wise and grand. But in truth he was neither of these things. Mr Twit was a twit. He was born a twit. And now, at the age of sixty, he was a bigger twit than ever. The hair on Mr Twit's face grew in spikes that stuck out straight like the bristles of a hairbrush. And how often did Mr Twit wash this bristly, nail-brushy face of his? The answer is NEVER, not even on Sundays. He hadn't washed it for years.

Figure 2b. (Words found: 16%)

Mr Twit was --- -- ----- ---- ---------- ---. --- ----- -- --- ---- ------ --- --- --------, --- ---- --- --- ---- was ------- ---- ----- ----. Mr Twit ---- ---- --- --------- ---- --- ---- ---- --- -----. --- -- ----- -- was ------- -- ----- ------. Mr Twit was - twit. -- was ---- - twit. --- ---, -- --- --- -- -----, -- was - ------ twit ---- ----. --- ---- -- Mr Twit's ---- ---- -- ------ ---- ----- --- -------- ---- --- -------- -- - ---------. --- --- ----- --- Mr Twit ---- ---- -------, ---------- ---- -- ---? --- ------ -- -----, --- ---- -- -------. -- ----'- ------ -- --- -----.

Figure 2c. (Words found: 43%)

Mr Twit was --- of ----- ---- ---------ed ---. The ----- of -is ---- ------ --- -is --------, -is ---- --- -is ---- was -----ed ---- ----- ----. Mr Twit ---- ---- -is -------- ---- --- ---- ---- --- -----. --- -- ----- he was ------- of ----- ------. Mr Twit was a twit. He was ---- a twit. --- ---, at the --- of -----, he was a ------ twit ---- ----. The ---- -- Mr Twit's ---- ---- -- ------ --at ----- --- -------- ---- the -------- of a ----brush. --- --- ----- --- Mr Twit ---- --is -------, ---------- ---- of -is? The ------ is -----, --- ---- -- -------. He ----'- ----ed -- --- -----.

Figure 3a. Concordance to 'de' in a text by Marcel Proust

1	ois en sapin ciré, qu'un violoniste	de ce pays lui avait donné et qu'elle
2	que les fidéles avaient l'habitude	de lui faire de temps en temps, afin q
3	les avaient l'habitude de lui faire	de temps en temps, afin que les donate
4	ue les donateurs eussent le plaisir	de les reconnaître quand ils venaient.
5	Aussi tâchait-elle	de persuader qu'on s'en tînt aux fleur
6	et c'était chez elle une collection	de chauffe-pieds, de coussins, de pend
7	le une collection de chauffe-pieds,	de coussins, de pendules, de paravents
8	tion de chauffe-pieds, de coussins,	de pendules, de paravents, de baromètr
9	fe-pieds, de coussins, de pendules,	de paravents, de baromètres, de potich
10	oussins, de pendules, de paravents,	de baromètres, de potiches, dans une a
11	dules, de paravents, de baromètres,	de potiches, dans une accumulation de

12	de potiches, dans une accumulation de	redites et un disparate d'étrennes.

Figure 3b. Put back in order the context on the right

1	ois en sapin ciré, qu'un violoniste de	baromètres, de potiches, dans une a
2	que les fidèles avaient l'habitude de	ce pays lui avait donné et qu'elle
3	les avaient l'habitude de lui faire de	chauffe-pieds, de coussins, de pend
4	ue les donateurs eussent le plaisir de	coussins, de pendules, de paravents
5	Aussi tâchait-elle de	les reconnaître quand ils venaient.
6	et c'était chez elle une collection de	lui faire de temps en temps, afin q
7	le une collection de chauffe-pieds, de	paravents, de baromètres, de potich
8	tion de chauffe-pieds, de coussins, de	pendules, de paravents, de baromètr
9	fe-pieds, de coussins, de pendules, de	persuader qu'on s'en tînt aux fleur
10	ussins, de pendules, de paravents, de	potiches, dans une accumulation de
11	ules, de paravents, de baromètres, de	redites et un disparate d'étrennes.
12	e potiches, dans une accumulation de	temps en temps, afin que les donate

Figure 3c. Find the missing word

1	Mr Twit was one of these very	y-faced men.
2	nd his nose was covered with thick	. Mr Twit felt that his hairiness m
3	Mr Twit felt that his	iness made him look wise and grand.
4	The	on Mr Twit's face grew in spikes t
5	ut straight like the bristles of a	brush.
6	As you know, an ordinary un	y face like yours or mine simply ge
7	But a	y face is very different.
8	Things cling to	s, especially food.
9	s like gravy go right in among the	s and stay there.
10	e or less all right again, but the	y man cannot do that.
11	But not the	y man.
12	atch carefully next time you see a	y man eating his lunch and you will

Figure 3d. Find the verbs ending in *-ait*

1	Mme Verdurin ----ait	assise sur un haut siège suédois en
2	qu'un violoniste de ce pays lui ----ait	donné et qu'elle conservait, quoiqu
3	nciens qu'elle avait, mais elle ----ait	à garder en évidence les cadeaux qu
4	détruisent ; mais elle n'y ----ait	pas, et c'était chez elle une colle
5	s elle n'y réussissait pas, et ----ait	chez elle une collection de chauffe
6	De ce poste élevé elle ----ait	avec entrain à la conversation des

7 conversation des fidèles et ----ait de leurs "fumisteries" mais depuis
8 ies" mais depuis l'accident qui ----ait arrivé à sa mâchoire elle avait ren
9 était arrivé à sa mâchoire elle ----ait renoncé à prendre la peine de pouff
10 de pouffer effectivement et se ----ait à la place à une mimique convention
11 ue ni risques pour elle, qu'elle ----ait aux larmes.
12 Au moindre mot que ----ait un habitué contre un ennuyeux ou co

Figure 4a. Concordance to the 'suffix' *-y* in *The Twits*

1 Mr Twit was one of these very hairy-faced men.
2 Twit wash this bristly, nail-brushy face of his?
3 As you know, an ordinary unhairy face like yours or mine sim
4 As you know, an ordinary unhairy face like yours or mine simply gets
5 hairy face like yours or mine simply gets a bit smudgy if it is not wash
6 urs or mine simply gets a bit smudgy if it is not washed often enough, a
7 But a hairy face is very different.
8 But a hairy face is very different.
9 Things cling to hairs, especially food.
10 Things like gravy go right in among the hairs and sta
11 go right in among the hairs and stay there.
12 faces with a flannel and we quickly look more or less all right again,
13 less all right again, but the hairy man cannot do that.
14 But not the hairy man.
15 Watch carefully next time you see a hairy man eatin
16 carefully next time you see a hairy man eating his lunch and you will n
17 hat, even if he opens his mouth very wide, it is impossible for him to g
18 e of this, Mr Twit never went really hungry.
19 Mr Twit never went really hungry. By sticking out his tongue and curling
20 ing it sideways to explore the hairy jungle around his mouth, he was abl

Figure 4b. Concordance to 'ly', whole sentences

1 As you know, an ordinary unhairy
face like yours or mine simply gets a bit smudgy if it is not
washed often enough, and there's
nothing so awful about that.
2 Things cling to hairs, especially food.
3 You and I can wipe our smooth
faces with a flannel and we quickly look more or less all right again,
but the hairy man cannot do that.
4 Watch carefully next time you see a hairy man
eating his lunch and you will

notice that, even if he opens his
mouth very wide, it is impossible
for him to get a spoonful of
beef-stew or ice-cream and
chocolate sauce into it without
leaving some of it on the hairs.

5 Because of this, Mr Twit never
went really hungry.

6 What I'm trying to tell you is that
Mr Twit was a foul and smelly old man.

7 He was also extremely horrid...

Figure 5a. The umbrella man by Roald Dahl and French translation: Concordances to the articles 'a' and 'un'/'une'

1	X01A I'm going to tell you about a	funny thing that happened to my mot
2	X02A I am twelve years old and I'm a	girl.
3	X06A It was in a	back tooth and he filled it without
4	X07A After that we went to a	café.
5	X08A I had a	banana split and my mother had a cu
6	X08A I had a banana split and my mot a	cup of coffee.
7	X11A "We must get a	taxi" my mother said.
8	X18A We stood on the pavement in the a	taxi.
9	X20A "I wish we had a	car with a chauffeur" my mother sa
10	X20A "I wish we had a car with a	chauffeur" my mother said.
11	X21A Just then, a	man came up to us.
12	X22A He was a	small man and he was pretty old, pr

1	X07F Après celà nou sommes allées	un salon de thé.
2	X08F J'ai pris	un banana split et ma mère a pris une
3	X11F "Il faut que nous prenions	un taxi" a dit ma mère.
4	X14F Je voulais encore	un de ces bananas splits.
5	X18F Nous étions sur le trottoir sou	un taxi.
6	X21F Juste à ce moment-là,	un homme s'est approché de nous.
7	X22F C'était	un petit homme et il était assez vieux

1	X01F Je vais vous raconter	une drôle d'histoire qui nous est arriv
2	X02F J'ai douze ans et je suis	une petite fille.
3	X05F Il a trouvé	une carie.
4	X06F C'était dans	une dent du fond et il l'a plombée sans
5	X08F J'ai pris un banana split et ma	une tasse de café.

6			X20F "J'aimerais avoir une voiture avec chauffeur" a dit ma m

Figure 5b. Right context to 'a' in alphabetical order

3	X06A It was in	a	back tooth and he filled it without
5	X08A I had	a	banana split and my mother had a cu
4	X07A After that we went to	a	café.
9	X20A "I wish we had	a	car with a chauffeur" my mother sa
10	X20A "I wish we had a car with	a	chauffeur" my mother said.
6	X08A I had a banana split and my mot	a	cup of coffee.
1	X01A I'm going to tell you about	a	funny thing that happened to my mot
2	X02A I am twelve years old and I'm	a	girl.
11	X21A Just then,	a	man came up to us.
12	X22A He was	a	small man and he was pretty old, pr
7	X11A "We must get	a	taxi" my mother said.
8	X18A We stood on the pavement in the	a	taxi.

Figure 6a. Parallel between the contexts of the English and French indefine articles in *The umbrella man.*

	01A I'm going to tell you about	a	funny thing that happened to my mother and me yesterday evening.
	01F Je vais vous raconter	une	drôle d'histoire qui nous est arrivée hier soir, à ma mère et à moi.
	A I am twelve years old and I'm	a	girl.
	02F J'ai douze ans et je suis	une	petite fille.
***	05F Il a trouvé	une	carie.
	06A It was in	a	back tooth and he filled it without hurting me too much.
	06F C'était dans	une	dent du fond et il l'a plombée sans me faire trop de mal.
	07A After that we went to	a	café.
	07F Après celà nous sommes allées dans	un	salon de thé.
	08A I had	a	banana split and my mother had a cup of coffee.
	08A I had a banana split and my mother had	a	cup of coffee.
	08F J'ai pris	un	banana split et ma mère a pris une tasse de café.
	08F J'ai pris un banana split et ma mère a pris	une	tasse de café.

	11A "We must get	a	taxi" my mother said.
	1F "Il faut que nous prenions	un	taxi" a dit ma mère.
***	14F Je voulais encore	un	de ces bananas splits.
	18A We stood on the pavement in the rain, looking for	a	taxi.
	18F Nous étions sur le trottoir sous la pluie, nous cherchions	un	taxi.
	20A "I wish we had	a	car with a chauffeur" my mother said.
***	20A "I wish we had a car with	a	chauffeur" my mother said.
	20F "J'aimerais avoir	une	voiture avec chauffeur" a dit ma mère.
	21A Just then,	a	man came up to us.
	21F Juste à ce moment-là,	un	homme s'est approché de nous.

Figure 6b. The three different cases:

05A He found **one** hole
05F Il a trouvé **une** carie.

14A I wanted **another** of those banana splits.
14F Je voulais encore **un** de ces bananas splits.

20A I wish we had a car with **a** chauffeur, my mother said.
20F J'aimerais avoir une voiture avec chauffeur ...

Figure 7a. 'Likes'

John doesn't like cooking, writing letters or classical music, but he likes tea with lemon, black coffee, whisky, Coca-Cola, sunbathing, detective films, jazz, rock music and spiders. He can't play the piano, repair things or drive a car, but he can play tennis, swim, ride a moped, dance and speak English. At school, his favourite subject is sports. Finally, his favourite hobby is basketball.

Isabel doesn't like whisky, Coca-Cola, jazz or spiders, but she likes tea with lemon, black coffee, cooking, sunbathing and rock music. Isabel thinks writing letters, detective films and classical music are all right. She can't play the piano or drive a car, but she can play tennis, swim, repair things, ride a moped, dance and speak English. At school, her favourite subject is sport. Finally, her favourite hobby is skiing.

Bella doesn't like black coffee, whisky or spiders, but she likes tea with lemon, Coca-Cola, sunbathing, writing letters and rock music. Bella thinks cooking, detective films, jazz and classical music are all right. She can't play the piano, play tennis, repair things or drive a car, but she can swim, ride a moped, dance and speak English. At school, her favourite subject is Greek. Finally, her favourite hobby is listening to music.

Figure 7b. 'Likes' information, with identification removed

--- doesn't like tea with lemon, whisky, sunbathing or jazz, but --- likes Coca-Cola, writing letters, detective films, classical music and spiders. --- thinks black coffee, cooking and rock music are all right. --- can't play the piano, play tennis, repair things, ride a moped, drive a car or dance, but --- can swim and speak English. At school, --- favourite subject is German. Finally, --- favourite hobby is drawing.

--- doesn't like tea with lemon, but --- likes black coffee, whisky, Coca-Cola, cooking, sunbathing, writing letters, detective films, classical music, rock music and spiders. --- thinks jazz is all right. --- can't play the piano or repair things, but --- can play tennis, swim, ride a moped, drive a car, dance and speak English. At school, --- favourite subject is mathemathics. Finally, --- favourite hobby is listening to music.

--- likes black coffee, whisky, Coca-Cola, sunbathing, rock music and spiders. --- thinks tea with lemon, cooking, writing letters, detective films, jazz and classical music are all right. --- can't play the piano, repair things, drive a car or speak English, but --- can play tennis, swim, ride a moped and dance. At school, --- favourite subject is sport. Finally, --- favourite hobby is dancing.

Figure 8a. *L'invitation au voyage*, mask

Mon [enfant], ma [soeur],
[Songe] à la [douceur]
D'aller là-bas [vivre] ensemble!
[Aimer] à loisir,
[Aimer] et [mourir]
Au [pays] qui te [ressemble]!

Figure 8b. *L'invitation au voyage*, part of the database

enfant	soeur	Songe	douceur	vivre	Aimer	mourir
amante	frangine	Clame	lourdeur	fuir	Hurler	partir
amie	poupée	Offre	frayeur	rire	Pleurer	sortir
bel ange	fleur	Dis	rondeur	luire	Lutter	subir
amour	femme	Apprends	pâleur	lire	Jouer	bleuir
bambin	tendre	Pense	laideur	rompre	Parler	mollir
chérubin	vie	Prêche	pudeur	naître	Crever	cueillir
aimée	douce	Crie	langueur	choir	Nager	courir
archange	puce	Renonce	douleur	plaire	Voler	venir
trésor	blonde	Commande	raideur	croître	Saluer	blondir
minou	chère	Laisse	rigueur	suivre	Semer	brunir
poussin	brune	Rêve	stupeur	vaincre	Céder	mentir
chaton	fière	Pleure	froideur	croire	Sauter	jaunir

Figure 8c. *L'invitation au voyage*, some sample 'automatic poems'

Mon fils, ma fille,
Renonce à la rigueur
D'aller là-bas rompre ensemble!
Manger à loisir,
Voler et mollir
Au vallon qui te retient!

Mon amante, ma chère,
Laisse à la stupeur
D'aller là-bas perdre ensemble!
Pleurer à loisir,
Semer et jaunir
Au pays qui te restaure!

Mon archange, ma rousse,
Songe à la rigueur
D'aller là-bas suivre ensemble!
Crever à loisir,
Rêver et sortir
Au rocher qui te sépare!

Mon chaton, ma fleur,
Rêve à la raideur
D'aller là-bas suivre ensemble!
Voler à loisir,
Hurler et courir
Au château qui te restaure!

Mon chaton, ma fille,
Soupire à la pudeur
D'aller là-bas perdre ensemble!
Céder à loisir,
Jouer et subir
Au sommet qui te retarde!

Mon poussin, ma fiére,
Prêche à la laideur
D'aller là-bas vaincre ensemble!
Créer à loisir,
Saluer et bleuir
Au torrent qui te sillonne!

Figure 9.

COMPUTER RAINBOW

Will life be as lucky for me
as it is today?
Will History be upstairs?
Will I be by the river?

I'd like to be as hard as you,
as fair as the swallows in the park.
Will I thank as far as you?
What will October bring?

Look at the onions in the traffic.
Can they miss Geography?
Will they ask me how to sleep?
I don't want to wait too long.

COMPUTER RAINBOW

Will life be as fair for me
as it is today?
Will the score be in the tube?
Will I be far away?

I'd like to be as cheap as you,
as soft as the peas in the kitchen.
Will I sleep as far as you?
What will Sunday bring?

Look at the creatures at the back.
Can they borrow the towel?
Will they ask me how to score?
I don't want to wait too long.

COMPUTER RAINBOW

Will life be as good for me
as it is today?
Will Mom be on the shelf?
Will I be in outer space?

I'd like to be as nervous as you,
as dangerous as the planets by the sea.
Will I sleep as far as you?
What will Wednesday bring?

Look at the stamps on the moon.
Can they miss the supper?
Will they ask me how to go?
I don't want to wait too long.

COMPUTER RAINBOW

Will life be as kind for me
as it is today?
Will English be on the bus?
Will I be in the bathroom?

I'd like to be as nervous as you,
as kind as my friends at the back.
Will I ride as far as you?
What will Thursday bring?

Look at my friends in the garden.
Can they cut the traffic?
Will they show me how to hurry?
I don't want to wait too long.

Recent Experiences in Large-Scale Computer-Assisted Instruction

James Pankhurst

0. INTRODUCTION

I am enthusiastic and sceptical about computer-aided education at the same time. Computers obviously have tremendous potential, simply because they are infinitely more flexible than any other educational technology that has come our way. But we are in the most initial and primitive stage with respect to their use. What I have to report is the experience of having prepared a course in English grammar on the computer, a course which would require the average student to spend 12 to 15 hours at the computer, which has been used by some one hundred students, with considerable evidence of success, which is now being used independently of me by other staff, and which is good enough for us to want to improve upon rather than to forget about. I am concerned here with issues like personal involvement of the author, the software package used, an account of what is involved in preparing courseware of this kind, and finally, how the students responded to the course.

1. PERSONAL INVOLVEMENT

The Utrecht Faculty of Letters set up an interdepartmental group known as Computer and Letters in 1985. The fact that the first noun was in the singular did not perhaps augur well. One area of concern was to be the development of computer-aided instruction. It was very much the poor relation amongst a number of research projects, but it did mean that there was a very small number of people released from other duties to work on specific educationally oriented programs. In my case, I was able to spend some nine months on my project on a half time basis. I was appointed to the task on the basis of my supposed didactic skills rather than on account of any computer expertise; the aim was to preserve, or to immortalise, good teaching in the form of a permanent computer program. This is a relevant comment, because an important question to be asked is the extent to which the author's personality can enter into computer-aided instruction. When I started work I had to learn how to use the authoring system we had decided on. I had tremendous support from the beginning but it was only after a considerable period of time that I had available on a full time basis a computer on which I could actually develop the material. I provide these details simply to point out that the amount of real time that went into the developmental work was not all that great.

The system I employed, TAIGA, developed at the Technical University of Twente, is simple to use and does not require any great computer expertise, but it takes as long to become fluent in it as it does to become fluent in any programming language. The advantage is that once one can use it comfortably, material can be prepared at a very much greater speed than any other way. One only becomes fluent in the system as a result of using it, so it is difficult to make an overall estimation of how long it takes to learn. However, once reasonable fluency is attained, it will take between 15 and 30 hours to prepare one hour of lesson time on the computer. Estimates like this are always dangerous. I tend to be optimistic, and this is less than the general prediction, which varies between 50 hours and 150 hours. Obviously, a lot depends on whether one is going to make use of sophisticated graphic presentations or not. My own estimate is in terms of what I consider to be fault-free material of an adequately high standard for internal use.

2. THE SOFTWARE PACKAGE

A TAIGA course can consist of up to 10 modules, each module being divided into 10 paragraphs of 10 episodes each. An episode is intended to encode a single interaction between the student and the computer; there are 49 steps available for any one interaction; steps include such basic functions as clearing the screen, or one part of the screen, presenting text, or a graphics frame, accepting a student answer, checking whether it is correct or analysing it with the question processor, recording the answer, updating counters, branching according to whether a student has supplied an appropriate response or not, and so on. It is extremely easy to set up a course with full menu selection by students, to introduce controls on what the student may progress to, it is easy to record for each student the time that has been spent working, the results achieved on particular exercises, and any other information that the course constructor sees as relevant. Current thinking in the circle I was working in was that students should be free to choose what they do, but be relatively constrained once they have made their initial choice. This was initially reflected in our courses by giving students menu-freedom, but constraining them to complete the designated tasks within the units they had selected. Such freedom is more illusory than real because the student is not likely to wish to embark on exercises which are in advance of his present ability; but it does provide good revision possibilities. On the other hand, I eventually became convinced that setting up a program with TAIGA that made students relentlessly pursue a hard exercise to the bitter end was no good thing. It was necessary to re-look at the material I had produced and see whether I could put the student totally in control of his exercises. It took some serious re-organisation to really let a student be in charge of deciding whether he was going to complete an exercise, whether he wanted to work out the answers himself, or whether he wanted the computer to tell him.

There are skills to be learned in order to produce courseware with any authoring system. As well as the basic manipulation of the facilities, there is good layout practice to be learned for the screen, which is one of the most important skills. There is the length of exercises, the level of difficulty, the avoidance of monotony. I have used the system regularly for several months, and while I am satisfied with the results, I am very conscious that what I am producing is still at a very non-professional level. The material presently available reflects various particular stages in my thinking about what is useful, and indeed in my ability to use the system.

3. BUILDING UP A COURSE

What does one aim to do when faced with the challenge of providing computer-aided instruction? You choose a subject which is done by a large number of students, where each student will benefit from individual attention, where they will have to make individual decisions, which can fairly easily be checked. First year grammar was an obvious choice, a subject I had been teaching for many years, but was not actually teaching at the moment. I had to fit in with someone else's approach to the course. I was to provide exercise material, which would support information delivered in the lecture. There was no question of doing without a teacher. In fact, since there were so many uncertainties in this first year, we had a system where the lecture was given, and where it was supported by tutorials and by work in the computer practicum. I was very conscious of the need to be relevant to students, also of the fact that it might be the case that not all students would have access to the computer practicum, and so I decided to make my exercises a mirror image of the material in the Workbook being used by the course. There are seven courseware disks, and the first four have exercises which correspond in a formal sense to exercises in the Workbook by Aarts and Aarts (1982), so that students could choose to work from the book or from the computer, or indeed both. The advantage of using the computer was that there would be an immediate notification as to whether they had got an answer right, and in almost all cases there would be an explanation of why the answer was right. I would like to stress very much that I find one of the most valuable aspects of this course the feedback as to why an answer was right or wrong. Another advantage – not present in all exercises yet – is the HELP facility. If a student does not know how to go about an exercise or a particular question, he can call up help, and he will be able to read a few essential notes, see a couple of key examples, and return to his exercise.

There are numerous organisational decisions to be made about the program: what sort of a scoring system is to be used, what kind of reinforcement will be available, how the HELP system will work, how the student will know where he is. And with all the facilities that TAIGA offers, it is still a complex and monotonous business to make exercises perfect, tidy and effective. Initially there is the desire to make use of as many as possible of the computer's facilities.

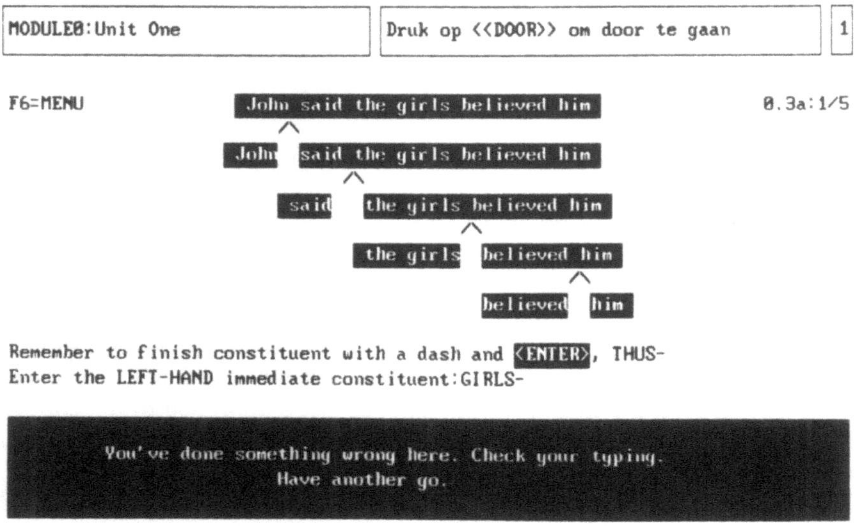

An early exercise (fig. 1) demonstrated how students could construct trees on the screen, based on an exercise in Aarts and Aarts (1982). This exercise was challenging to make, it looks quite impressive, but students did have minor problems actually following out the instructions, and that, of course, is something that one wants to avoid completely.

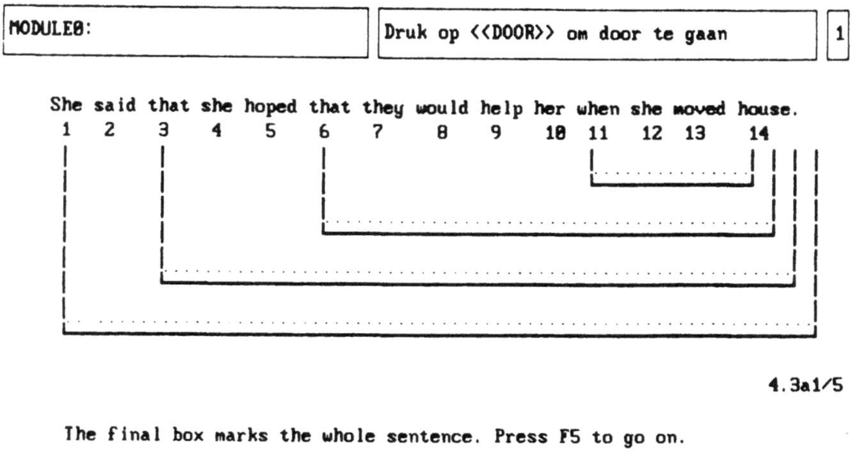

A later example of trying overfaithfully to mirror the Workbook exercises is the attempt in fig. 2 to identify embedded clauses. I am not saying it was bad, what I am saying is that at this stage in my own development, in an attempt to fit in with an existing course, I was constraining myself unnecessarily.

These more visual displays tended to be the exception rather than the rule in the initial stages. Some inventiveness worked, and some didn't. For example, there is one exercise where students are asked to put constituency brackets around relatively simple sentences. That kind of exercise may be okay on paper, but it is not fun doing it on a keyboard. Eventually, I settled down to a more or less stable format whose main advantage should have been, and I suppose was, that there was individualised feedback for every single question.

The regular format obviously has tremendous advantages as far as planning is concerned, because once one has obtained a satisfactory format, one can go on at a very good speed producing material. In fact, using this standard format one can really work fast. But it became too dull for the students, so I became a bit more adventurous with my sentences, and sent John and Mary down to the local, where they had adventures, and got drunk on tomato juice, engaged in betting on the horses, and generally got involved in all kinds of cultural activities. I larded the grammatical comments with the cultural, or sometimes with the purely humorous. This certainly worked much better. Then the next stage was to abandon the Workbook. Originally my exercises had faithfully reflected it, because we did not really know how many computers we would have available, and had to be seen to be giving all students the same course. But now we had 64 computers, and any student who wanted to could go along and work with the diskettes. So I started asking myself why I did not simply produce useful exercises, and forget about the book. That is what I tried to do in my final three disks. One very basic activity that all students need to be good at is dividing a sentence up into its elements, and giving category and function labels. This I felt was the real thing, and again, once the general set-up had been worked out, it was surprisingly easy to produce material. I even found a way of dealing with discontinuous constituents, although I do not think it ideal. This was the first disk to really allow the student the freedom to ask the computer to give him the answers. He is "charged" extra penalty points for this service. But this exercise was still not the real nitty gritty. The real challenge would be to be able to ask students to give a full tree analysis for sentences. Well, my final production achievement was to do this. The technical solution suddenly came in the middle of the night. As is usually the case on computers, the tree is drawn sideways. The maximum length of sentence is 17 words, and the level of embedding is reasonable, but limited by the width of screen. To analyse a 17 word sentence students have to make about 80 decisions as to constituent division, categorial and functional labels. The initial screen contains only the sentence itself, for which they are asked to indicate the first constituency division, and after some time the tree begins to build up, until finally there is a complete tree, and the student is invited to ask for a printout, as in fig. 3.

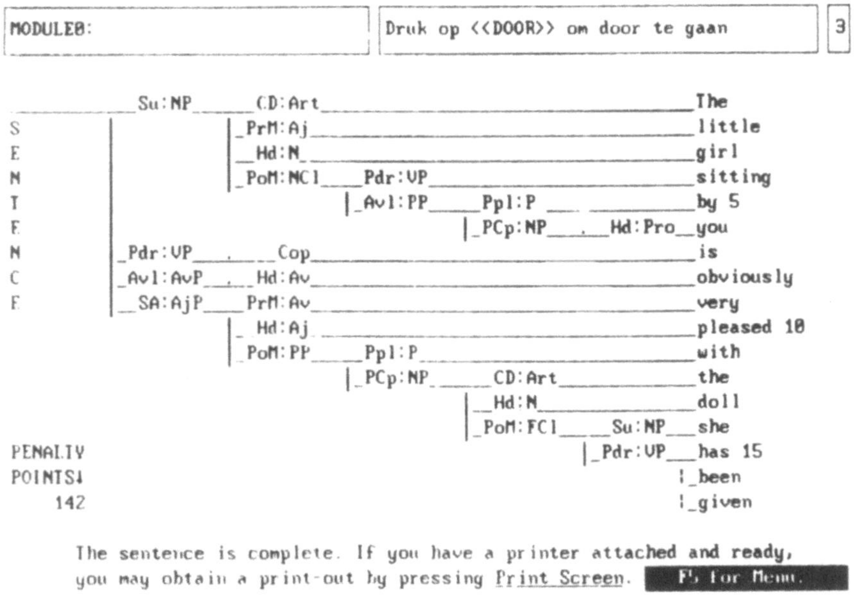

What I have tried to describe is my own approach to developing material. I have not mentioned the problem of obtaining feedback on how students were working. There is a way of filing any information on performance that you want. I used it, but not optimally. I have not talked about the technical problems of making the disks trouble free runners. There were occasional disk errors, and even one or two program errors, but these were so small as not to be a cause of concern. All I want to do now of course is to rewrite the course, to make it my own rather than parasitic on another lecturer and another course book. I feel I have learnt enough to have a go at producing something much more professional, and hopefully more useful. The question arises as to how successful this was in relation to students.

4. STUDENT REACTIONS

Most, but not all students, were delighted to work on computers, and regarded it as a privilege rather than a bind. Inevitably, in spite of their having full written instructions, they needed some assistance on the first day, but after that they really did manage on their own, and we found that it was not necessary to have a student assistant on hand the whole time. We are at present studying their reaction to the course, and evaluating their responses to it; at the moment full data are not available, but it appears that although the practicum aspect of the course was in addition to the tutorials, rather than an essential part of the course, half of all first year students completed the whole course, taking between 7 and 15 hours to work through the seven courseware disks. There is clear evidence of learning in that initial scores for particular exercises are sometimes low, while repeats of the same exercises produced much better scores. One of the most remarkable aspects is the tremendous differences in speed between students. It is quite common for some to take three times as long as others to do the material. Obviously, in some cases they were just talking rather than working, but clearly, the computer does and can allow people to work at their own speed in a way that is impossible in tutorials. It was particularly interesting to notice the records for the full sentence analysis. It took students between 20 minutes and an hour to analyse one sentence. Most of them did all three full analyses, and if they obtained sixty penalty points in the first attempt, they reduced this to half in their third attempt. Penalty points were awarded one for each wrong answer, but also two for every request to be given an answer. We cannot separate these two counts out, but quite obviously, students preferred to work things out for themselves rather than simply have things done for them. Otherwise, their penalty points would have been much higher than in fact they were.

We asked students which exercises they preferred and why. While these questionnaires have not yet been fully processed, it is easy to give a picture of the sort of replies. For example, I myself was somewhat surprised to hear that a student liked what I thought was a rather boring exercise on relative and appositive clauses. I asked what was so attractive about it, and was told that the explanations were so clear and helpful, suggesting indeed that one might risk more teaching (and not simply practising) on the computer. Then I was taken down a peg or two by a student who told me that without any doubt the very worst exercise was the full tree analysis, the exercise that I myself thought was the very apex of my achievement. There were special factors; this particular student had already been in the practicum two hours before starting that exercise, but I realised that from the students' point of view, they were plunged straightaway into the lengthy analysis of 17 word sentences, with accurate, but rather confusing instructions. Obviously, this kind of exercise may be good, but it needs a lead-in.

I am now faced with making an honest evaluation of my efforts in terms of time and money invested in the past and to be invested in the future. One thing is clear, that whether we are talking about administrative systems being computerised or research, or teaching, the initial costs are enormous, they are beyond my comprehension, and I take it as given that the computers are there, that they are to be used. Then, I can say with no doubt in my mind at all that it will be more than well worth my while to continue, to revise and improve my programs. I see what I have already produced as valuable in the context of the course, and I know truly how much better I could make it, and I am also able to say that I can improve and update it in a reasonable amount of time. I am also enthusiastic enough about the whole system to want to share my experiences with colleagues, to encourage them to learn TAIGA, and so on.

5. CONCLUSION

A more interesting title for my paper might have been Nightmares and Dreams. Maybe it doesn't sound that nightmarish – I have not mentioned how I felt when a whole week's work was destroyed in one electronic crash, or about my frustration when told that the Faculty had spent so much on computers that they had no money left to buy floppy disks. Or about the tedium. There is no short cut to inputting your sentences, making up good feedback, and checking everything thoroughly. I finished producing the course just before Christmas, just ahead of the students who completed the course just after Christmas, but much midnight oil was burnt in order to have the final disk working in time. Possibilities for using the computer in many aspects of our English program are continually presenting themselves. One thing is clear: the challenge is there, the rewards in terms of teaching satisfaction are great, and we will be able to go on learning how to improve our CALL software for a long time to come.

REFERENCE

Aarts, F. and J. Aarts. 1982. *English Syntactic Structures Workbook*, Pergamon Press, Oxford

ZICOM: An Application of the Authoring System AMOR

Lucie Huiskens
Peter-Arno Coppen

0. INTRODUCTION

This paper contains an introduction to the authoring system AMOR (Section 1) and a description of ZICOM, a major application of AMOR (Section 2).

AMOR is a general purpose authoring system for programming series and networks of questions and follow-up questions. The flexibility and powerful answer evaluation possibilities of AMOR allow not only for the definition of closed questions: it can even handle half-open questions.

ZICOM is an application of AMOR, in which a complete tutoring program is defined for sentence analysis. ZICOM is mainly Dutch-oriented. However, a sentence analysis tutor for any language can be designed in accordance with the same procedures.

Current implementations of the two programs run on an IBM-370 mainframe with operating system VM/CMS and on IBM(-compatible) PCs with operating system MS-DOS. The MS-DOS implementation needs at least 256 K RAM, and two disk drives or a hard disk. For AMOR only, just one disk drive is enough.

1. THE AMOR AUTHORING SYSTEM

In this section the main features of the AMOR authoring system for MS-DOS personal computers will be discussed. AMOR is a text-oriented authoring system for various environments, which defines a special small programming language for asking questions, evaluating answers and displaying feedback or providing more detailed information.

The AMOR language consists of a few commands for programming a tutoring device. This language is entirely in Dutch, but for practical reasons the English translation will be used in this paper[1].

Although the AMOR language is fairly concise, this paper cannot be read as a user manual. Only a few general ideas will be touched upon, and some concrete examples will be given of a typical application of AMOR.

1.1 The structure of AMOR

In a grammar class a teacher typically confronts his students one by one with several well-chosen questions to check which student has acquired the desired knowledge or skills, and which student needs feedback and/or further practice. The answers of each student to the questions asked give the teacher an indication of his skills. Very often, though, student answers remain vague and incomplete. In a classroom situation, such answers may prompt the teacher to ask follow-up questions, in order to find out whether an incomplete answer signals lack of knowledge or skill or results from misunderstanding the question. Furthermore, follow-up questions are also used to teach the student a particular strategy for finding the answer to the original question. For instance, suppose a student does not know how to find the grammatical subject in a sentence. The teacher who tries to explain how this task is to be performed will have to point out that locating the finite verb in the sentence is the first step to do this. After this has been done, the agreement between the verb and one of the constituents in the sentence has to be determined. The constituent agreeing with the finite verb is the grammatical subject.

So, schematically we can distinguish between original questions (called TASKS) and follow-up questions. The teacher will confront the students with a series of TASKS, and if necessary, will ask follow-up questions, until the original task is performed.

The structure of the AMOR authoring system reflects this general idea. A typical application of AMOR consists of a series of TASKS, and an unordered set of follow-up questions. The system confronts the student with the tasks consecutively, and on some occasions (determined by the answers given by the student), AMOR branches to follow-up questions specified in the application. From there, branching is allowed to any other follow-up question, until the original task is performed. AMOR then proceeds to the next task.

In principle, the student who immediately performs all the tasks correctly, will not be confronted with follow-up questions. However, the teacher, or the designer of the program, may decide to ask certain follow-up questions anyway.

1.2 Answer evaluation

Student answers to questions, as noted before, may be vague or incomplete. Any adequate computer program trying to simulate classroom situations has to account for that. This means that it is inadvisable to offer the student a choice from a limited list of answers (multiple choice), or ask for a yes-or-no answer (Y/N) and leave it at that. Adequate computer systems will have to allow for answers that are neither completely correct nor completely wrong. A student who does not know the exact answer, will often have a hunch about the sort of answer he should give. He should have the opportunity to show this hunch, so that the teacher can react to it, and the student does not have to start the whole procedure again. If a minor error results in him having to repeat the entire procedure, the student will get frustrated and will consequently refrain from giving answers he is not completely sure of. This will slow down the learning process.

As a consequence, computer systems simulating classroom situations will have to be very flexible in evaluating answers. For each question, the correct answer has to be determined (with some degree of tolerance), but the teacher who designs the computer system has to anticipate expected errors as well. Each type of error has to trigger a specific type of feedback, and, if necessary, branching to specific follow-up questions.

The AMOR system is designed to cope with this problem. The general outline of answer evaluation offers the teacher an unlimited number of tests to evaluate the answer. The first test that succeeds determines the action AMOR will take. Schematically, the structure of answer evaluation can be represented as follows:

IF	**the answer is such-and-such,**
THEN SAY	**specific feedback**
AND BRANCH TO	**follow-up question**
IF	**the answer is so-and-so**
THEN SAY	**some other feedback**
AND BRANCH TO	**another follow-up question**
etcetera...	

The number of tests that the teacher can specify is not limited by AMOR but, of course, purely practical considerations may force him to set a limit.

The evaluation of the answer may contain a number of tests, each of which examines a particular aspect that determines a specific type of feedback or branching.

In each test, one condition can be evaluated. This conditon can be simple or complex. Again, there is no theoretical limit to the complexity of the condition. Perhaps the simplest condition is the condition on the form of the answer:

IF **ANSWER('LOUIS XIV')**

This condition tests whether the answer consists of the characters LOUIS XIV (no more, no less). A certain degree of tolerance can be built into the system by using the AMOR-primitive ARB (for ARBitrary):

IF ANSWER('LOUIS' ARB)

This condition tests whether the answer begins with the characters LOUIS, followed by an arbitrary (possibly empty) string of characters. This condition will be fulfilled if the answer is for example one of the following:

LOUIS THE SUN KING
LOUIS XIV
LOUIS THE BRAVE
LOUIS
LOUISIANA

The elements **'LOUIS'** and **ARB** together constitute a so-called PATTERN for the evaluation of the answer. The PATTERN concept, taken from SNOBOL (Griswold et al. 1971), offers a powerful means of evaluating the contents of string variables. The ARB primitive is just one of many examples. Another example is the possibility of disjunction:

IF ANSWER('LOUIS' ('XIV' | 'THE SUN KING'))

The above condition defines the strings:

LOUIS XIV
LOUIS THE SUN KING

And it reads: If the answer is **LOUIS**, followed by either **XIV**, or **THE SUN KING**, ... (The vertical bar (|) is the disjunction character).

A condition to be evaluated can be complex in its pattern, but it can also consists of several conditions:

IF ANSWER('LOUIS' ARB) AND NOT(ANSWER('LOUISIANA'))

This condition consists of two parts, one the already familiar condition testing for the occurrence of the characters **LOUIS** at the beginning of the answer, and the other prohibiting the acceptance of the answer **LOUISIANA**.

A condition can consist of two or more other conditions, combined by means of either conjunction (both conditions must be true), or disjunction (at least one of them must be true). That a complete test for a question is based on these simple principles is shown in the following example, where the answer should be **LOUIS XIV** (or equivalent).

```
IF          ANSWER('LOUIS' ('XIV' | 'THE SUN KING'))
THEN SAY    That is correct
AND BRANCH TO END
IF          ANSWER('LOUIS' ARB) AND NOT
IF          (ANSWER('LOUISIANA'))
THEN SAY    You picked the wrong LOUIS...
AND BRANCH TO follow-up question #1
ELSE
THEN SAY    You are not even close
AND BRANCH TO follow-up question #2
```

1.3 Parameterization

One of the main features of AMOR is the possibility to have parameters as part of the questions. Parameters can be looked on as variables determining the contents of, for instance, a question, a condition or feedback.

Suppose we want to ask questions about the sovereigns of several countries. We would then have to pose questions like:

Who is the sovereign of France?
Who is the sovereign of Spain?
Who is the sovereign of Belgium?

It would be a very tedious enterprise indeed to spell out essentially the same question for each country we want to know the sovereign of. AMOR offers a way to enter a parameter instead of the name of the country, so that no more than one question is needed:

QUESTION.1
Who is the sovereign of &COUNTRY?

(The ampersand in the text of this question indicates that COUNTRY is a parameter). The only thing we now need to do is to make sure that the same question is asked with different values of the parameter COUNTRY. This is where the TASK notion comes in.

We made a distinction between original questions (TASKS) and follow-up questions. The follow-up questions were called from both task questions and other follow-up questions, whereas the TASKS were asked consecutively. Now if we want to ask questions about the sovereigns of several countries, we can regard these questions as follow-up questions, called from different TASKS. Each TASK determines one particular country and calls the above parameterized question. E.g.:

```
TASK 1
COUNTRY          = 'France'
BRANCH TO        QUESTION.1

TASK 2
COUNTRY          = 'Belgium'
BRANCH TO        QUESTION.1
....etcetera
```

Now only QUESTION.1 (see above) is needed for the entire range of possible questions.

In each TASK we can define an arbitrary number of parameters that can be used in the follow-up questions called from that TASK. Parameters can be used in the following way:

(1) As variables in AMOR text (the text of questions, feedback)
(2) As variables in AMOR patterns

Consider the following TASK:

```
TASK 1
COUNTRY          = 'France'
CORRECT          = 'LOUIS' ('XIV' | 'THE SUN KING')
HALFCORRECT      = ('LOUIS ' ARB | 'LOUIS')
BRANCH TO        QUESTION.1
```

In this case QUESTION.1 could be something like:

QUESTION	**QUESTION.1**
:	**Who is the sovereign of &COUNTRY ?**
IF	**ANSWER(CORRECT)**
THEN SAY	**That is correct**
AND BRANCH	**TO END**
IF	**ANSWER(HALFCORRECT)**
THEN SAY	**You almost got it right**
AND BRANCH TO	**FOLLOW.2**
ELSE	
THEN SAY	**That is not correct**
AND BRANCH TO	**FOLLOW.1**

1.4 Conclusion

It is impossible to give a complete description of AMOR within the scope of this paper. We have only been able to give an outline of the system. Although the language of AMOR is concise and easy to understand, some practice is needed in order to be able to work with it. It is necessary to get acquainted with the means AMOR provides for the solutions of particular problems. An important advantage with respect to using AMOR is that AMOR is an interpretive language. This means that once a tiny bit of AMOR code has been written, the user can check his work so far with a few keystrokes.

This makes it easy to adopt a trial-and-error method in designing an AMOR application: the user can begin by specifying only major tests in his answer evaluation, first concentrating on the structure of the network of follow-up questions, and postponing the refinement of the answer evaluation until a later stage. Usually, the need for refinement in certain places will become clear only after extensive testing. In this way the user is encouraged to set up a 'rough' application first, and subsequently to test and refine the answer evaluations and the structure of the network.

2. ZICOM, A CAI PROGRAM FOR SENTENCE ANALYSIS

ZICOM, an application of AMOR, is a CAI program for sentence analysis. It allows the learner to practise grammar skills at his own level, applying the theory which has been outlined in class.

ZICOM has been designed to help the learner to adopt successful search strategies, which enable him to distinguish and identify the parts of the sentence in both simple and complex sentences (and, in the case of complex sentences, also the constituent clauses) and to assign words to word classes.

This implies that a correct answer is not immediately provided when the learner makes an error. Rather, follow-up questions help him to find the correct answer himself.

AMOR has been developed within SNOBOL. SNOBOL is a programming language which features a powerful pattern match. This makes it possible to circumvent, in a fairly simple way, the mechanical procedures typical of much educational software. For example, it allows ZICOM to deal very specifically with various aspects of the sentence under analysis during task performance. Moreover, a range of alternative answers is available to the learner. Yet, the program is relatively compact as well as efficient and easy to handle.

As ZICOM has been written in AMOR, it is easy for a teacher to adapt it to his own ideas or didactic methods. ZICOM has originally been developed to teach first year students of Dutch at the University of Nijmegen. This implies that it may be necessary to change some of the terminology in the program, when it is used for different populations, e.g. secondary school pupils.

The program contains about 350 parsing tasks, but it is fairly easy for a teacher to construct some more tasks if he wants to. In the next sections, examples will be given of the five component parts of ZICOM, in order to show that ZICOM is a system with which any teacher of grammar who can operate an editor can work.

All examples in this section were originally written in Dutch, but for the sake of convenience have been translated into English.

2.1 The five component parts of ZICOM

2.1.1 The task sentences

The task sentences constitute the basis of every parsing task; this part also contains the information necessary in processing the task. In each task sentence the word or word group to be analyzed is surrounded by %-signs in order to highlight it on the screen (when a monochrome monitor is used) or to display it in a contrasting colour. Furthermore, in each task sentence some variables have been assigned a value specific for that sentence. Here follows an example of this part of ZICOM:

```
Task DIR.OBJECT.2 @1
:       My neighbour has bought%a brand-new car%; I wonder how he
:       can afford it?! /
PHRASE = 'a brand-new car'
DECLINE = 'has'
VARTIME = 'My neighbour%had%bought a car'
VARNUMBER = 'My neighbours%have%bought a car'
DECLINE2 = 'can'
PREDICATE = 'has bought'
VARSUBJ = 'my neighbour'
NUMBERTEST = '%my neighbours have bought%a car'
WHTEST = 'What has my neighbour bought? %a brand-new car%'
OTHERSENT = 'I wonder how he can afford it'
THISSENT = 'my neighbour has bought a brand-new car'
CONTROL = DIR.OBJ
CODE = 'CLEFT.DIR.OBJ'
BRANCH TO GENERAL.1
```

The lines beginning with a colon contain the task sentence itself. The word group to be analyzed (**a brand-new car**) is a direct object.

GENERAL.1 is the task question which belongs to this (kind of) task (cf. AUX.TIME.1 in 2.1.2).

The words to the left of the equal sign are the variables, the lines to the right of it their values. Some of these variables are used in examining the answers, others in commenting on the answer: if used with an ampersand (&) their values will be displayed, not their names, as is shown in the next example, taken from a training session with ZICOM.

The first two lines constitute the task sentence, in which the word group in bold type is the topic of the task; the third line is the first follow-up question in the network; the fourth line is the answer the learner has given, the remaining lines are ZICOM's comments on this answer. (NB: for practical reasons, this example is different from a real screen display in ZICOM):

> My neighbour has bought **a brand-new car**; I wonder how he can afford it?!
>
> What is the finite form in this sentence?
>
> CAN
>
> '**can**' is a finite form all right, but not in the sentence to which '**a brand-new car**' belongs. That sentence is:
> **My neighbour has bought a brand-new car**
> Try again...
>
> ==> press RETURN for the next question

The follow-up question in this example is posed after the student has given an incorrect answer to the question 'what part of speech is '**a brand-new car**''; the student should know that the phrase 'this sentence' refers to the sentence containing '**a brand-new car**'.

The words in bold type are the result of the value assignment to variables: in the original text of the comments the variables are preceded by the ampersand and thus, on the screen, the current value is displayed. In this way each question can be used several times in different situations, while it remains possible to go into the details of the sentence under analysis.

2.1.2 The task questions

The task questions focus on a part of a sentence and contain the so-called evaluations-of-the-answers, comments on the answers and, if necessary, a branch to a follow-up question. Each task question contains the texts of the question and of a series of tests on the answer.

The next example illustrates the use of answer evaluation in which different kinds of errors are anticipated. Note the parameter **PHRASE** for which the current value will be substituted when this question is displayed on the screen. This means that this question can be used in all tasks about auxiliaries.

```
Question AUX.TIME.1
:               What part-of-speech is %&PHRASE.%in the task
:               sentence?
IF              ANSWER(CONTROL)
THEN SAY That is correct!
AND BRANCH TO END
IF              ANSWER(AUXILIARY)
THEN SAY        That is partly correct.%&PHRASE.% is indeed a
THEN SAY        &Answer., but you have to elaborate on this.
AND BRANCH TO VERB.4
IF              ANSWER(SPECIFIED.AUX)
THEN SAY        That is not correct. %&PHRASE.% is an auxiliary
THEN SAY        all right, but &Answer. is the wrong type.
AND BRANCH TO AUX.1
IF              ANSWER(VERB)
THEN SAY        You are right in that %&PHRASE.% is a verb, but
THEN SAY        your answer does not suffice...
AND BRANCH TO EXTRA.VERB
IF              ANSWER(SPECIFIED.VERB)
THEN SAY        That is not correct. Although %&PHRASE.% is a verb,
THEN SAY        it is not a &Answer.
AND BRANCH TO VERB.1
IF              ANSWER(QUESTION)
THEN DISPLAY HELP.PARTOFSPEECH
IF              ANSWER(PATTERN.DECLINE)
THEN SAY        &Answer is the name for one of the%declinations%
THEN SAY        of the verb. Yet you were asked to denote
THEN SAY        %&PHRASE.% as a part-of-speech. Please try again...
AND BRANCH TO AGAIN
IF              ANSWER(GRAMM.FUNCTION)
THEN SAY        &Answer denotes a grammatical function. Please
THEN SAY        denote %&PHRASE.% as part-of-speech.
AND BRANCH TO AGAIN
IF              ANSWER(PART.OF.SPEECH)
THEN SAY        That is not correct. The following questions will
THEN SAY        teach you how to find the correct answer.
AND BRANCH TO BASIC.2
```

Lines beginning with **'IF'** are the actual tests.

IF ANSWER(AUXILIARY) means: does the answer match the pattern AUXILIARY (which will be the case if the answer is the string 'auxiliary' or any abbreviation of it). The lines beginning with **'THEN SAY'** contain the text that will be displayed on the screen if the preceding test has succeeded. Lines beginning with **'AND BRANCH TO'** contain a branch to another question or to END. The latter means that the task has been completed.

This example shows that various possible student errors can be anticipated within these tests, but any teacher is free to put in additional tests, or leave certain tests out, by editing the file containing this question. There is no limit to the number of tests: the greater the number of tests, the more specific feedback can be provided, the more the specific need of each individual student can be catered for.

2.1.3 The follow-up questions

The follow-up questions form a network of questions teaching the student how to find the correct answer. It simulates, in a way, the steps taken by an expert when solving a problem of syntactic analysis. The follow-up questions and the task questions are essentially similar; the difference is that the former are part of a network. Where the student enters this network depends on the error he has made.

The following example shows one of the follow-up questions which belong to the series of questions about the adjunct:

```
Question ADJUNCT.1
:            Does%&PHRASE.%belong to a sentence element?
IF           ANSWER(QUESTION)
THEN DISPLAY HELP.ADJUNCT1
IF           ANSWER(YES) AND
IF           ITS.ABOUT(PART.OF.SENT.ELEMENT)
THEN SAY     That is correct.
AND BRANCH TO ADJUNCT.2
IF           ANSWER(NO) AND
IF           ITS.ABOUT(ADJUNCT.IN.POST.POSITION)
THEN SAY     That is not correct,%&PHRASE.%
THEN SAY     could very well be seen as a part of the sentence
THEN SAY     element: %&CONST.%/
AND BRANCH TO ADJUNCT.2
IF           ANSWER(NO) AND
IF           ITS.ABOUT(PART.OF.SENT.ELEMENT)
THEN SAY     That is not correct,%&PHRASE.%
THEN SAY     is a part of the sentence element %&CONST.%/
AND BRANCH TO ADJUNCT.2
IF           ((ANSWER(YES) Print('That is not correct.')), OR
IF           (ANSWER(NO) Print('That's true.')))
THEN SAY     /%&PHRASE.%
THEN SAY     is an independent sentence element and therefore
THEN SAY     it can't be an adjectival adjunct....
AND BRANCH TO ADJUNCT.4
```

A test like:

IF ANSWER(YES) AND ITS.ABOUT(PART.OF.SENT.ELEMENT)

succeeds when the answer is 'yes' and the word group in question belongs to a sentence element.

Note that this test can be used for adjectival adjuncts (because then it will succeed and the comments that go with it will be displayed) as well as for adverbial adjuncts (then it will fail, and the next test will be executed).

This particular question ADJUNCT.1 belongs to a network which handles the three kinds of adjuncts that are distinguished in Dutch grammar. It contains all the steps that have to be taken in order to arrive at the right conclusion. The learner can be led to this question via two ways: If his answer to the task question is adjunct, which is incomplete, the next question he will get is this one. But if his answer is totally wrong, he will first have to answer a series of questions about the finite verb in the sentence, about the subject, the object, etc. Depending on the skills he has already acquired the learner will be able to skip some steps in the network (and eventually to give the right answer at once).

This is a fairly natural way of learning: first the solution is shown step by step, then certain steps can be skipped, until, finally, the correct answer can be given at once, without going into details.

The follow-up questions can be adjusted in the same way as the task questions. In fact, if a teacher decides that some distinctions do not have to be made by his students, he may decide to remove entire 'branches' from the network.

2.1.4 The patterns

All grammatical terms and other possible answers the student might give are defined in a grammar. This approach has two advantages: 1) the student can phrase his answers in the terms he is used to; he can even give incomplete answers, and 2) ZICOM can check the answers in detail.
In the next example the numerals are defined:

```
DEF = ('DEFINITE' | 'DEF') ('.' | ' ')
INDEF = ('INDEFINITE' | 'INDEF') ('.' | ' ')
------ Numerals ------
NUMERAL = CARDINAL | ORDINAL | COUNT
CARDINAL = DEF.CARDINAL | INDEF.CARDINAL
ORDINAL = DEF.ORDINAL | INDEF.ORDINAL
DEF.CARDINAL = DEF CARDI
INDEF.CARDINAL = INDEF CARDI
CARDI = 'CARDINAL' | 'CRDNL'
DEF.ORDINAL = DEF ORDI
INDEF.ORDINAL = INDEF ORDI
ORDI = 'ORDINAL' | 'ORD'
COUNT = 'NUMERAL' | 'NUM' | 'NUMER'
```

These patterns are used in the examinations-of-the-answer. Suppose the next test succeeds:

IF ANSWER(CARDINAL) AND ITS.ABOUT(DEF.ORDINAL)

This means that the student knows that the part of speech in question is a NUMERAL, but he cannot distinguish between the two kinds of numeral (he answers *cardinal* whereas the part of speech under analysis is a *definite ordinal*). At this moment the learner is referred to a network of questions which teach him how to make the right distinction.

If, however, the next test succeeds:

IF ANSWER(COUNT) AND ITS.ABOUT(NUMERAL)

then the only possible conclusion is that the answer is incomplete. Here only a reference to a question for a more specific answer is in order. If the answer to this question should be wrong, then the reference to the network can be made after all.

A question in which the answers are evaluated in this way can be used in tasks for different kinds of NUMERALS; this contributes to the efficiency of the system. It is even possible to define a pattern with which it can be checked whether the student is not sure about the correctness of his answer. This could be the case if he adds something like 'I think' or words to that effect to his answer. When that happens, the system could ask for more details, or it could give more detailed comments. In this way, the training program imitates regular classroom teaching even better.

2.1.5 The instructions

Before answering each question, the learner can ask for instructions: that part of the theory which is necessary for answering the question will be displayed on the screen. This facility has been built into the system because quite a few grammatical terms or notions are used in the follow-up questions, and, although these have been explained in class, the student might not know exactly what they mean. In order to answer a question about the finite form, for instance, the learner has to know what is meant by a finite form. If he does not know, he can ask for help by entering a question mark, or by answering something like *I don't understand*. This will cause the following information screen to be displayed:

FINITE FORM
The finite form (FF) is the finite verb in the sentence.
There are two possible ways to find the FF:
(1) by changing the tense of the sentence.
The verb that changes is the FF. E.g:
-We **want** to go to the zoo today -->
We **wanted** to go to the zoo yesterday

(2) by changing the number of the subject of the sentence.
Then the FF changes, too. E.g:
-They **want** to go to the zoo -->
He **wants** to go to the zoo

==> Press RETURN to return to the question

After studying this information the student returns to the question to have a second go at it.

3. CONCLUDING REMARKS

In this paper, the authoring system AMOR and ZICOM, a major application of this system for the teaching of sentence analysis, has been described. ZICOM has been used at the Dutch Department of the University of Nijmegen since 1985. First-year students can work with it when(ever) they like, but it is not an obligatory part of the grammar course. Nevertheless, most students prefer to practise their sentence analysis skills with ZICOM. They also tend to spend more time on sentence analysis than they would without ZICOM. They think it is more fun than working at home with a book, because they get immediate feedback on their answers. Moreover, exam results have been influenced positively.

During the past two years, several institutes have bought AMOR and ZICOM. Some of them, especially teacher training colleges, use AMOR not only for developing applications for their own teaching, but also for teaching teacher-trainees how to use CAI programs in school, and how to develop them themselves.

Recent developments include AMOR applications for the teaching of some aspects of English grammar to Dutch learners. AMOR applications need not be restricted to the domain of language learning: at the moment an application for the teaching of law is being developed at the University of Nijmegen.

NOTE

1. The English AMOR version described in this paper will be available for those interested. As a matter of fact, the AMOR language can be translated very easily into any other language.

REFERENCE

Griswold, R., J. Poage and I. Polonsky. 1971. *The SNOBOL4 Programming Language*, 2nd edition, Prentice Hall, Englewood Cliffs, N.J.

On Developing a Sentence Analysis Program: A Progress Report

Nico Robat

0. INTRODUCTION

In this paper I wish to report on the development of a computer program currently undertaken in the English Department of the University of Groningen and directed at providing first-year students of English with additional or remedial practice with the syntactic analysis of sentences in a CAI-setting.

First, I shall briefly sketch the organisation of the project. Then I shall describe the type of program we are developing, concluding with a report on what has been achieved so far and what still remains to be done.

1. ORGANISATION

The CAI-project that I want to report on is called CASA. It is a small-scale sentence analysis program, which has been funded by the University of Groningen since January 1985. It is one of two CAI-projects that the Groningen Department of English is currently involved in, the other one (VOCAL) being a vocabulary acquisition project. Both research projects are aimed at exploring the possibility of incorporating CAI into our curriculum.

In September 1985, after the green light had been given to start both projects (each for the duration of three years), we invited students to share in the work by participating in a seminar course devoted to the development of the CASA-project. The response we got from students was considerable, and the format has since proved to work most satisfactorily. The students are very keen and the week-to-week work on the syntax program has benefited in no small way from their contributions.

The work is done in collaboration with the Groningen Centre for Research in Higher Education: COWOG. This centre has put at our disposal the services of a systems analyst, whose task it is to translate the models proposed by us into an acceptable computer program. On top of these facilities the University allowed us to appoint a temporary part-time research assistant.

In this paper I shall focus exclusively on CASA, the sentence analysis program.

2. THE DESIGN OF CASA

In the preliminary talks with COWOG it soon became clear that the partners were in full agreement over the general requirements of the program to be developed. It had to be intelligent, interactive and user-friendly – for both student and administrator, that is. This meant, for one thing, that we envisaged a program that needed only the briefest of instructions before a student could begin the first session in front of the machine, and also software which could be added to or changed without it being necessary to call in the help of a qualified programmer.

A factor of crucial importance was COWOG's condition that in this new age of austerity the costs of developing the program should be firmly kept under control. So, right from the start, it was understood that designing a program catering exclusively for the needs of English sentence analysis was quite out of the question. Instead, it was proposed to try and produce a type of program from which a number of versions could be derived, the prerequisite here being that with each new application it should be possible to break down the specific learning task on similar lines. In other words, the partnership aimed for a product that could be adjusted not only to the requirements of certain types of language instruction, but also to those of comparable activities in, say, econometrics or pharmacy.

This objective was served by opting for a design having as its core a binary tree representing a hierarchically structured sequence of decisions which an expert is assumed to take in the process of solving an analytic problem. Since this type of program driving CASA is applicable whenever such a process can be represented by a decision tree or a network of such trees, the scheme was considered a viable proposition in terms of production costs.

The program is written in C, a language somewhat reminiscent of PASCAL. A strong reason for selecting C, and not a typical authoring system such as TAIGA or a CAI-language like PILOT, was that with this language it is possible to maintain a strict separation of the data and the program operating on the data. Other attractive features of this modular language are that writing in C makes it easy to transfer the entire program from an IBM-compatible to another machine, that C is increasingly becoming an industry standard and also a standard for developing CAI-software, while, in addition, it is a high-level language accessing all the hardware of the machine it runs on.

The program contains two different text files, which can be changed by anyone who can handle a word processor. One file comprises all the sentences (in analysed form) which are offered as practice material. The other file contains the information and help options. The program governing when and how the various questions, infos etc. are presented on the screen is divided into several parts, of which the core can only be changed by an expert programmer. By contrast, the other parts such as the (sub)trees and the way in which these trees are called up can be modified by a non-expert. While the program is running, the student has access to help options, which can also be changed without the assistance of a skilled programmer.

Having decided on the type of program, we considered how this approach could be profitably related to the syntactic descriptions as presented in the textbook which is used for the syntax course taught in years I and II of our curriculum. This teaching grammar, Van Ek and Robat, *The Student's Grammar of English* (*SGE*) presents in the opening chapters a fairly traditional, middle-of-the-road description of English sentence structure in the Quirkian vein.

We first set out to design a program for the simple sentence, and we began with the identification of the syntactic functions of sentence elements (in the *SGE* framework: the phrases). In accordance with the original plan, we constructed a single decision tree representing the hierarchy of decisions relating to function classification as presented in chapter 1 of *SGE*, together with the set of subtrees specifying the various functions. These subtrees were next incorporated into the appropriate places in the main tree.

However, after we had worked along these lines for some time, we felt the need to slightly modify the original concept. A strong claim for the single decision tree had been that if an incorrect answer was given, it would be possible to trace where in the tree the student had taken the wrong turning, so to speak. Remedial work was then to be undertaken proceeding from the student's last correct decision. Apart from the trouble it had given us to regiment the functional framework of *SGE* into one single tree (admittedly a lesser problem), we doubted whether the tree truly reflected the procedure followed by an expert. Also, there was the serious problem that if the incorrectly identified function was far below the correct one, the student would have to be taken through a series of less relevant questions to point out the error.

For these, and other reasons, we modified the rigidly vertical structure of the binary tree by introducing a two-stage representation, the first stage being represented horizontally as follows:

This corresponded more closely to the description of sentence structure as given in the introductory chapter of *SGE*, which, within the predicate, distinguishes between obligatory and optional elements. In addition, this approach was more direct and still allowed us subsequently to introduce the various subtrees for complement and optional: the second stage.

3. CASA AS IT NOW STANDS

The program as we now have it presents the student with a sentence and asks him or her to identify the function of an underlined element by selecting the appropriate label from the menu. When a question is answered correctly, the student goes on to the next question, and that is all there is to it. It is when problems arise over function identification, however, that the fun starts. Briefly, the program can now do one of two things:

- it can explain why a certain answer is wrong by leading the student through the tree of the incorrectly identified function, thus leading to the conclusion '... and therefore not X'. The student is then invited to try again.
- it can guide the student to the correct answer by taking him or her to the tree of the appropriate function, thus leading to the conclusion '... and therefore X'.

If in a practice session the answer given is wrong, and the problem concerns the identification of subject or predicator, the student is led straightaway to the subject tree or the predicator tree in order to guide him or her to the correct identification. The motivation for this procedure is that we feel that elementary mistakes of this kind call for immediate action.

If the mistake is within COMPL (e.g. X is direct object, not subject attribute) or within OPT (e.g. X is vocative, not adverbial), the student is first shown why his or her answer is wrong and is then invited to try again. Should the student next fail again, he or she is taken to the tree of the appropriate function.

If the mistake can be attributed to confusion over the distinction between optional and obligatory elements (e.g. X is adverbial, not adverbial complement), the student is first shown this aspect of the mistake and then invited to try again. Should the student fail again, he or she is taken to the tree of the appropriate function.

This is perhaps the place to give an example of how the program handles problems. Let us assume that the line *All the girls go for accordeon Joe* is presented on the screen and that the question is to identify the function of the sequence *All the girls*.

If our imaginary student selects – say – the function label 'direct object', the program qualifies the answer as wrong and, since the mistake has to do with 'subject', it takes our student to the subject tree (see Appendix 1).
Since the program must also cater for existential constructions, the first question on entering the subject tree now asked is:

'Is the underlined element the word *there*?'

Theoretically, the student can now give either 'Yes' or 'No'. If 'Yes', the program qualifies the answer as wrong, tells the student so, and presents the next question, which also follows the correct 'No':

'Is the underlined element repeated in a tag in the form of a personal pronoun?'

Again, either 'Yes' or 'No' can be answered. The correct 'Yes' is followed by the same question as the incorrect 'No', albeit it that in the case of the incorrect 'No', the student receives some information before he or she is presented with the next question:

'So what's the function of the underlined element?'

If the student now comes up with 'subject', we have reached the end of this road. However, if the student comes up with a function label other than 'subject', he or she is told that the answer is wrong, and the program next takes over, gives the correct function label and presents additional information on elements functioning as subject (see INFO 8, Appendix 2).

Here, then, the repetition of the subject in the form of a personal pronoun in a tag question is used as the distinguishing characteristic of the functional category under discussion. As can be seen in the subject tree, the same approach is used in the case of existential *there*. However, the procedure to arrive at the appropriate function identification of notional subjects in existentials differs. Here our criterion is the concord relation between the finite verb form and the noun phrase following the predicator.

At present the program only offers practice in function labelling. The student can either choose practice in labelling all the sentence elements in a set of sentences, or practice in identifying a particular function of his or her choice, for instance, predicator complement. We are in the process of extending the program with form class labelling, so that in the completed program for the simple sentence there will also be an opportunity for students to practise the identification of phrases and word classes. We are planning to insert an option which enables students to ask for information of an explanatory nature on grammatical terms and concepts used in the practice material (e.g. the student may feel uncertain about terms such as 'finite', 'tag', or 'personal pronoun'). This additional service, we think, will preclude unnecessary obstacles.

The program as it now stands can handle active and passive simple sentences, with the exception of interrogative structures. This has to do with the way in which we identify functions such as subject and direct object. The way in which we intend to compensate for this shortcoming is to include 'transformation exercises' in the program which require the student to turn declarative sentences into interrogative structures. It is to be expected that the skill to 'derive' certain types of sentences from a basic type – the declarative – will enable the students to successfully identify the syntactic function of elements in structures which are not handled in the program.

Finally it should be noted that in the practice sessions the student is shown by underlining what sequences of words constitute elements. In other words, the program in its present state does not address the problem of segmenting sentences. However, segmentation is bound to turn up in full force when in the remaining time of the project we direct our efforts to developing CASA into a program that can handle complex as well as simple sentences.

NOTES

1. I wish to thank Lucie Huiskens, Peter-Arno Coppen and Frans Schaars of the Dutch Department of the University of Nijmegen for their kind help and encouragement when we in Groningen were in the initial stage of our project, not quite knowing how we were to tackle the job at hand.
2. VOCAL: Vocabulary Computer Assisted Learning.
3. CASA: Computer Assisted Sentence Analysis.

REFERENCE

Van Ek, J. and N. Robat. 1984. *The Student's Grammar of English*, Blackwell, Oxford

Appendix 1

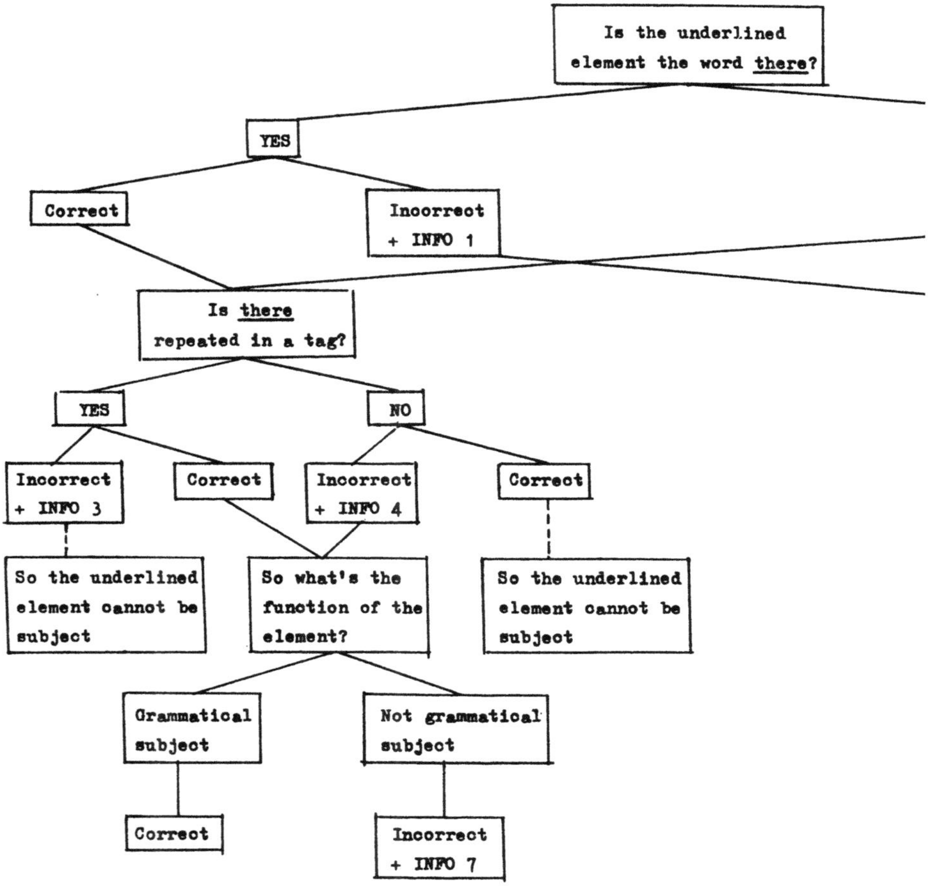
Is the underlined element the word there?
YES
Correct
Incorrect + INFO 1
Is there repeated in a tag?
YES
NO
Incorrect + INFO 3
Correct
Incorrect + INFO 4
Correct
So the underlined element cannot be subject
So what's the function of the element?
So the underlined element cannot be subject
Grammatical subject
Not grammatical subject
Correct
Incorrect + INFO 7

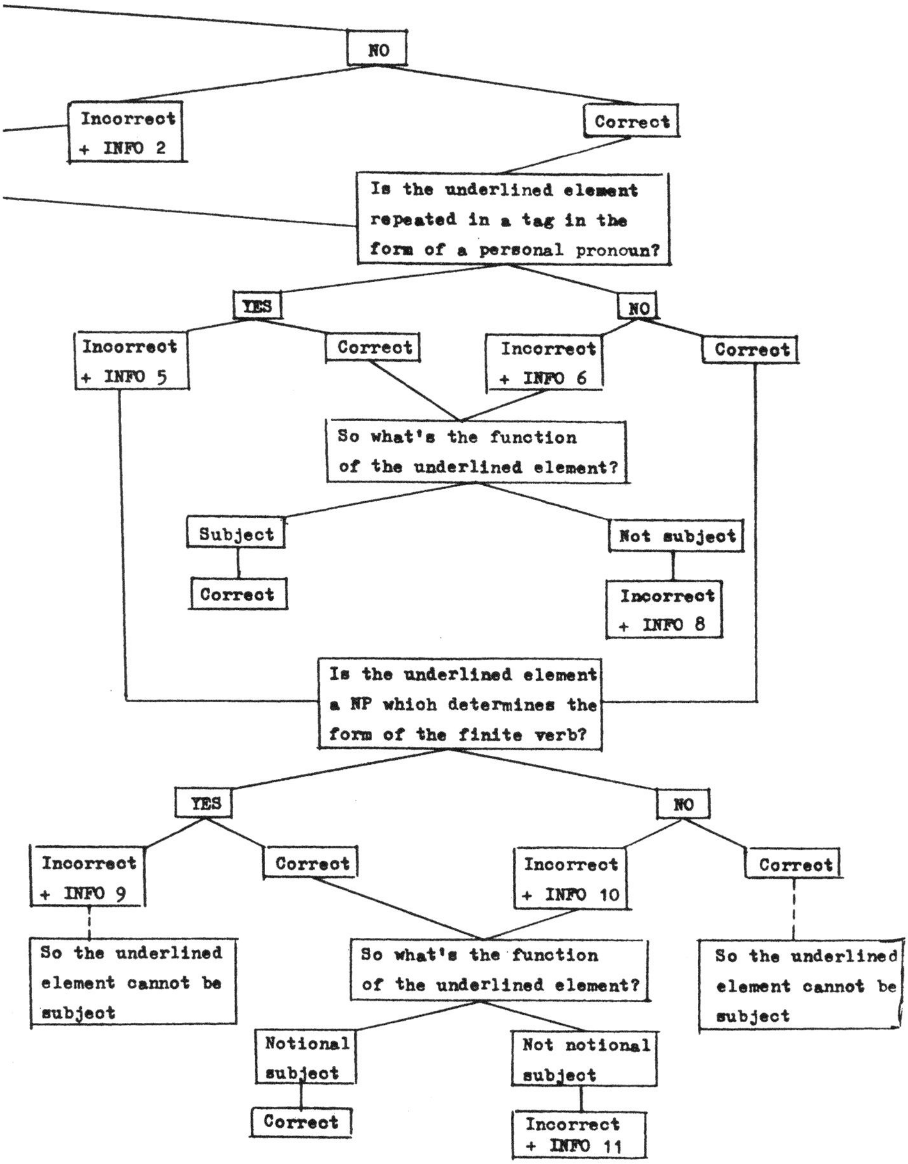
NO
Incorrect
+ INFO 2
Correct
Is the underlined element
repeated in a tag in the
form of a personal pronoun?
YES
NO
Incorrect
+ INFO 5
Correct
Incorrect
+ INFO 6
Correct
So what's the function
of the underlined element?
Subject
Correct
Not subject
Incorrect
+ INFO 8
Is the underlined element
a NP which determines the
form of the finite verb?
YES
NO
Incorrect
+ INFO 9
Correct
Incorrect
+ INFO 10
Correct
So the underlined
element cannot be
subject
So what's the function
of the underlined element?
So the underlined
element cannot be
subject
Notional
subject
Not notional
subject
Correct
Incorrect
+ INFO 11

Appendix 2

SUBJECT TREE: INFOS

1. You are wrong. Look again: the underlined element is not the word *there*.
2. You are wrong. Look again: the underlined element is the word *there*.
3. That is not correct. In the sentence you are analysing *there* is not repeated in a tag in the same way as illustrated in the following sentences:
   There were lots of people at your party, weren't there?
   There will not be another opportunity later this year, will there?
4. That is not correct. In the sentence you are analysing *there* is repeated in a tag in the same way as illustrated in the following sentences:
   There were lots of people at your party, weren't there?
   There will not be another opportunity later this year, will there?
5. Your answer is not correct. Consider the following sentence:
   John smiled, didn't he?
   In this sentence 'he' refers to 'John'. In other words, 'John' is repeated in the form of a personal pronoun in the tag. However, in the sentence you are analysing, it is not the underlined element that is repeated when you add a tag, but another element.
6. Your answer is not correct. When you add a tag, the personal pronoun in the tag refers to the underlined element in the same way as 'he' refers to 'John' in the following sentence:
   John smiled, didn't he?
7. Your answer is wrong. If *there* is repeated in a tag, it must function as grammatical subject.
   (Note that in this type of sentence there is also a notional subject.).
8. That is incorrect. If an element is repeated in a tag in the form of a personal pronoun, this element must be the subject.
   Other characteristics of elements functioning as subject are:
   - in statements this element precedes the verb phrase (e.g. Then *John* smiled).
   - in yes/no questions this element follows the first word of the verb phrase (e.g. Did *John* smile?)
   - the element functioning as subject may determine the form of the finite verb (e.g. You *are* early – He *is* early).
9. That is not correct. Consider the following sentences:
   The prisoner has escaped.
   The prisoners have escaped.
   In these two sentences the form of the finite verb is determined by the noun phrase that precedes it. If a singular NP ('prisoner') precedes

the finite verb, this verb has to agree in number: singular ('has'). If a plural NP ('prisoners') precedes the finite verb, this verb again has to agree in number: plural ('have'). In the sentence you are analysing the underlined element is not the element that determines the form of the finite verb.

10. Your answer is wrong. Consider the following sentences:

    There is a large hole in the bucket.
    There are several large holes in the bucket.

    In these two sentences the form of the finite verb is determined by the noun phrase that follows the verb phrase. The singular NP 'a large hole' determines the form of the finite verb: 'is'. The plural NP 'several large holes' determines the form of the finite verb: 'are'. In the sentence you are analysing the underlined element determines the form of the finite verb in the same way as illustrated here.

11. Your answer is wrong. In the sentence you are analysing there are two subjects: a grammatical subject *there* and a notional subject. You have already established that the underlined element
    - is not the word *there*
    - is not repeated in a tag in the form of a personal pronoun
    - determines the form of the finite verb

    So the underlined element must be the notional subject.

Possible Uses of Syntactic Analysis Trees in Syntax Teaching

Hans van Halteren

0. INTRODUCTION

The corpus linguistics group at the University of Nijmegen has developed a computer program for the exploration of syntactically analysed text-corpora (see Van Halteren and Oostdijk 1988), Van Halteren and Van den Heuvel (forthcoming). Two of the functions of this Linguistic Database are the presentation of syntactic analysis trees on a normal terminal screen and the selection of sentences with specified properties (see next section). The system was designed to be used by people without any experience with computers.

The Linguistic Database is the first computer program to present corpus data in this kind of detail. This, coupled with the ease of use and versatility of the system, has led linguists from all over the world to react enthusiastically to its arrival. Many suggested the possibility of adapting the system so that it can function as the practical component in a syntax course and this adaptation is now under way. The adapted system will not just be able to show examples, but will also contain a number of options for interaction in which the student is asked to point out or name certain structures. The normal mechanism for selecting sentences will not be available directly to the student, but he will have to use the selection criteria preprogrammed by the teacher. The new system is named Computer Library of Utterances for Exercises in Syntax (CLUES).

As CLUES has been adapted from the language independent Linguistic Database, it can be used for exercises on the syntax of any language. However, in this paper only English examples will be given. CLUES is aimed in the first instance at tertiary level education, but may eventually be adapted for use at secondary level. The first field test will be the second year syntax course for students of English at the University of Nijmegen. In 1988, the traditional oral exercise sessions will be replaced for the first time by computer sessions with CLUES.

1. THE LINGUISTIC DATABASE AS IT STANDS

Before exploring the possibilities of exercises with CLUES we will give an impression of how the Linguistic Database is currently used.

The Linguistic Database contains syntactic analysis trees. Each node of a tree represents a constituent of the analysed utterance and is labelled with information about that constituent: its syntactic function (e.g. subject), its syntactic category (e.g. noun phrase) and possibly some other attributes (e.g. third person, plural). At the leaves of the tree the words of the utterance are found.

An analysis tree can be examined on the terminal screen with the so-called Tree Viewer. The examination can be performed in two different modes, which are shown in figs 1 and 2 (These two and all following figures are exact copies of the screen contents during a session with CLUES). In the Tree Map View (fig. 1) only the structure of the tree is shown. The nodes are not labelled, but marked with their 'son number', i.e. the position they hold among all the immediate constituents of the dominating node. In the Environment View (fig. 2) only part of the tree is shown, but with every node on the screen the labelling is given, albeit in abbreviated form (see Appendix I for a list of the labels in the figure). In both modes one node, called the focus, is marked, and its labelling is shown in detail at the bottom of the screen. Commands are provided to move the focus through the tree and to scroll it in case it extends beyond the edges of the screen. At the bottom line of the screen all possible commands are listed in an abbreviated form (see Appendix II for a list of commands).

```
ON THE FAR SIDE OF THE LITTLE SQUARE THERE WAS A WALL WITH A PIERCED DECORATIVE
           ┌─1─ . . . . . . . . .   ON
           │       ┌─1─ . . . . . . THE
     ┌─1───┤       ├─2─ . . . . . . FAR
     │     └─(2)───┼─3─ . . . . . . SIDE
     │             │     ┌─1─ . . . OF
     │             └─4───┤     ┌─1─ THE
     │                   └─2───┼─2─ LITTLE
─*───┤                         └─3─ SQUARE
     ├─2─ . . . . . . . . . . . . . THERE
     ├─3─ . . . . . . . . . . . . . WAS
     │     ┌─1─ . . . . . . . . . . A
     │     ├─2─ . . . . . . . . . . WALL
     └─4───┤       ┌─1─ . . . . . . WITH
           │       │     ┌─1─ . . . A
           └─3─────┤     ├─2─ . . . PIERCED
                   └─2───┼─3─ . . . DECORATIVE
                         ├─4─ . . . BORDER
                         └─5───┬─1─ IN
                               └─2─ BRICKWORK.

PREPOSITIONAL COMPLEMENT:NOUN PHRASE
command:
scroll:YUDLR<>() focus:FS1-9OPNMJ view:V help:? exit:X
```

Figure 1: The Tree Map View

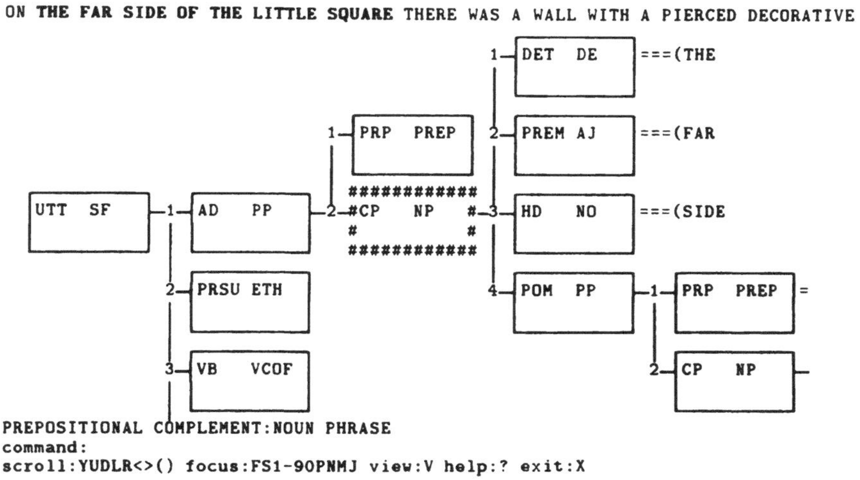

Figure 2: The Environment View

An analysis tree showing particular features can be tracked down within the corpus by means of a search pattern. In such a pattern, the user specifies a combination of nodes that have to be present in the desired analysis tree. With each node of the pattern properties are given for the corresponding node in the analysis tree and the connections in the pattern define the connections in the analysis tree. An example of a simple search pattern is shown in fig. 3. It describes a node with CATegory label Noun Phrase, having at least three immediate constituents, with the FUNction labels DETerminer, HeaD and POstModifier respectively. The utterance shown in figs 1 and 2 contains three such noun phrases, viz. 'THE FAR SIDE OF THE LITTLE SQUARE', 'A WALL WITH A PIERCED DECORATIVE BORDER IN BRICKWORK' and 'A PIERCED DECORATIVE BORDER IN BRICKWORK'. The matching nodes of the first occurrence are all shown in fig. 3. Note that in this case the noun phrase also has a PREModifier, which was not specified in the search pattern; not all the nodes need to be specified in the pattern, but only those that must be present.

Fig. 4 shows that such a pattern may get more complex. This pattern again searches for a noun phrase containing a determiner, a head and a postmodifier, but with some extra restrictions:

a) The determiner must not be the first constituent of the noun phrase (as the son number, SNO, is specified as being greater than 1).

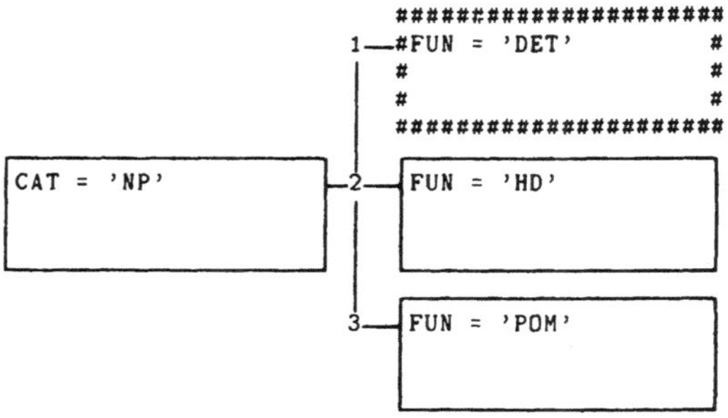


```
FUN = 'DET'
command:
scroll:YUDLR()<> focus:FS1-9OPN edit:IETCOW view:V help:? exit:X
```

Figure 3: A simple Search Pattern

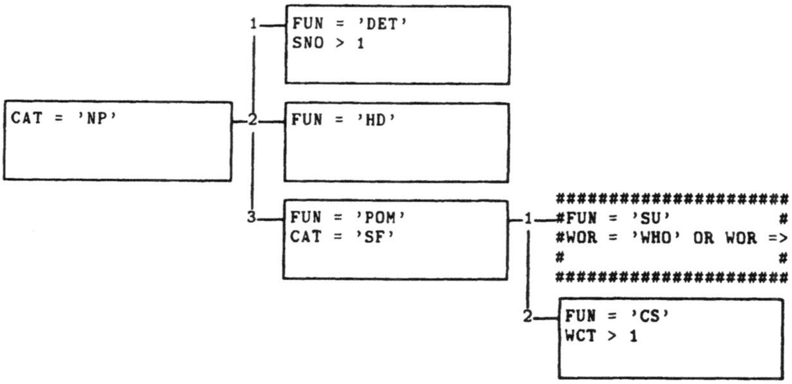


```
FUN = 'SU' ; WOR = 'WHO' OR WOR = 'THAT'
command:
scroll:YUDLR()<> focus:FS1-9OPN edit:IETCOW view:V help:? exit:X
```

Figure 4: A somewhat more complicated Search Pattern

b) The postmodifier has to be a finite sentence (SF) with a subject (SU) and a subject complement (CS).

c) The subject has to be realised by the relative pronoun 'WHO' or 'THAT'.

d) The subject complement has to consist of more than one word (WCT stands for word count).

An example of such a noun phrase, found in one of our corpora, is the subject of the utterance 'MANY A DOCTOR WHO IS SHY AND HESITANT IN PUBLIC DONS COMPLETE CONFIDENCE WITH HIS WHITE PROFESSIONAL COAT.'

2. EXERCISES WITH CLUES

A linguist using the Linguistic Database only examines trees. A student using CLUES, however, has to show that he understands the structure of the analysis tree under examination. This calls for some kind of question/answer system. The exercises described below indicate our current ideas in this matter. All these exercises are carried out within the Tree Viewer mentioned above, so that the student can examine every part of the analysis tree, except for some items which are hidden because of the role they play in the exercise. Also, for this occasion, the Tree Viewer is extended with extra commands for answering the questions posed. If more than one node is involved in the question, the normal focussing mechanism can be used to indicate which part of the question is being addressed. The student is not allowed to exit the Tree Viewer until the question is answered in full. For each exercise an example will be given, on the basis of the first noun phrase in the utterance of figs 1 and 2.

2.1 Exercises with a full tree

In the first set the exercises are restricted to node labelling. The syntactic structure is visible in its tree form.

A) Show examples, examination as only interaction

The first exercise is in fact no more than an examination of the example presented (cf. figs 1 and 2). It can be used in introducing new concepts to the student. Furthermore, in the first sessions with CLUES it helps the student to familiarise himself with the way in which the analyses are presented.

B) Mark node, ask for label

In the selected tree a node is marked (see fig. 5) and the student has to provide information about it. This could be the category of the constituent, but also its function within the next higher constituent or certain attribute values. Exercises in word class assignment can be done too, by concentrating on the leaves of the tree. Note that in the command list at the bottom of the screen an addition has been made. It mentions the three new commands needed for this exercise. Command Q (Question) repeats to the student what he is asked to do in this exercise. This may be necessary as the original instruction may have disappeared from the screen because of Tree Viewer operations. Command A (Answer) provides the correct solution for the student who cannot find it himself. In this exercise the labels that were hidden are revealed. The Tree Viewer is not yet exited as the student has to have an opportunity to examine the solution. The last new command is O (Open). With this command the student can open a node in order to place in it the label he thinks should be there. If the proposed label is correct, it remains in the node; if not, the student is told that he was wrong and the correct label remains hidden.

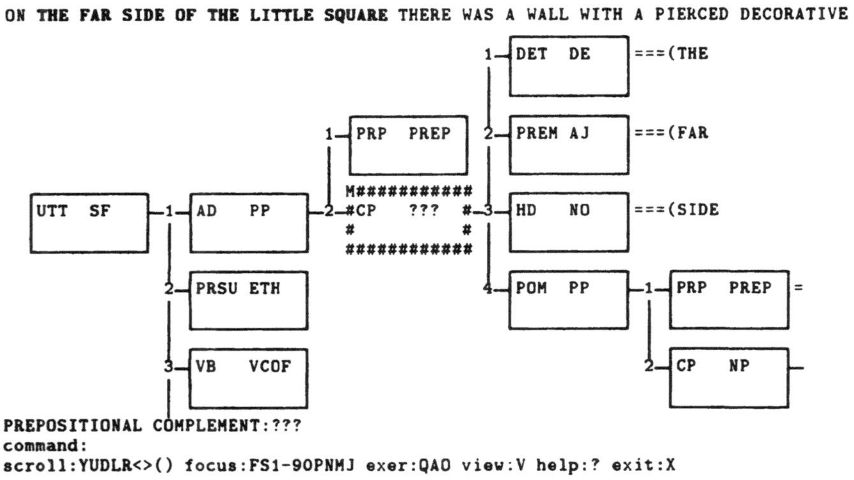

Figure 5: What category label is hidden by the question marks?

C) Give label, ask for node

The type of node in question (e.g. its category) is given (see fig. 6) and the student has to point out a node of that type, or all such nodes in the tree. As in the previous exercise, the information given can be category, function, attribute or word class. Commands Q and A have the same functions as in exercise B. The third command listed under 'exer' (exercise), however, is different from the third one in exercise B. The student is not asked to type in labels, but he has to indicate nodes. For this he is given command H (Here). In order to point to a node which he feels has the desired properties, he uses the normal focussing mechanism to move to it and then gives the command H.

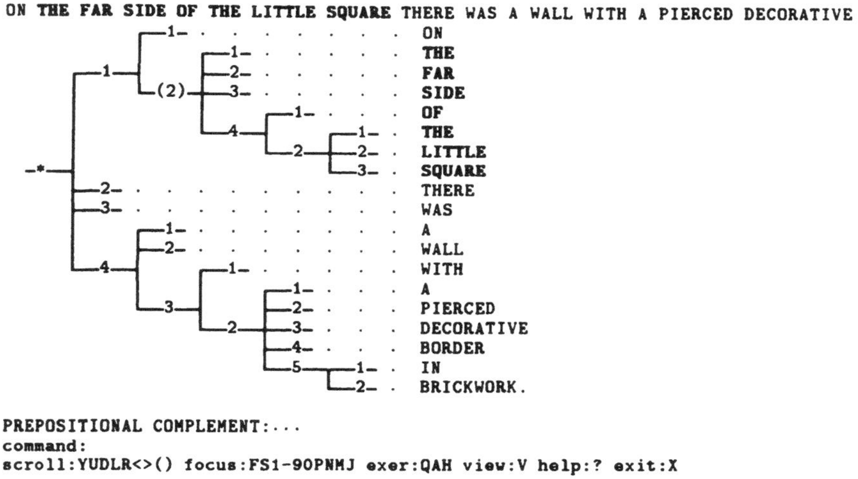

Figure 6: Indicate all nodes with category Noun Phrase

D) Mark area, ask for labels

Exercise B can be extended to more than one label and node. A possible use would be to have the student name the category of a constituent and its structure in the form of the functions of its immediate constituents (see fig. 7). An extreme form of such an exercise is to have the student fill in the entire tree.

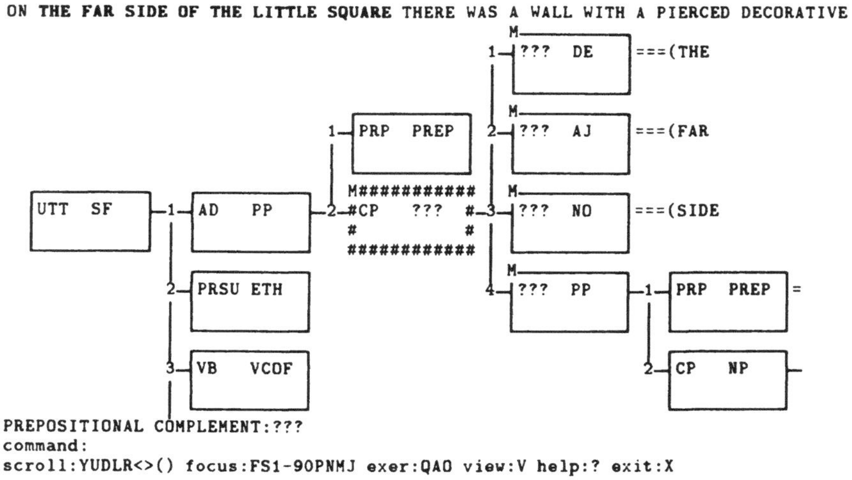

Figure 7: Which labels are hidden by the question marks?

E) Give characterisation, ask for node(s)

Exercise C can also be extended to a situation with more than one label or node. The student now has to point out the set of nodes that show the combination of labels provided (fig. 8).

```
ON THE FAR SIDE OF THE LITTLE SQUARE THERE WAS A WALL WITH A PIERCED DECORATIVE
```

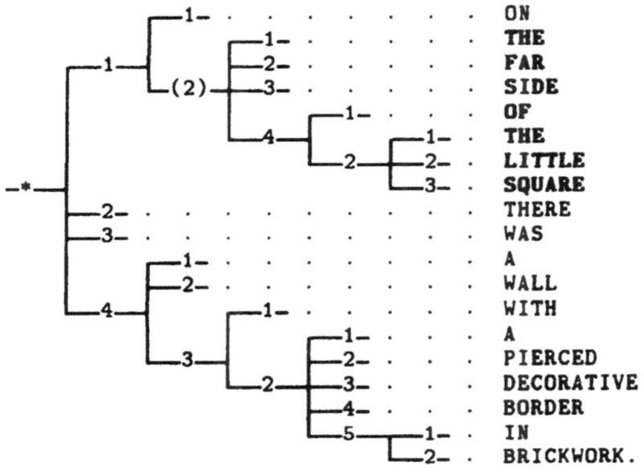


```
...:...
command:
scroll:YUDLR<>() focus:FS1-9OPNMJ exer:QAH view:V help:? exit:X
```

Figure 8: Indicate all Noun Phrases containing a Premodifier

2.2 Exercises with a mutilated tree

While exercises A to E leave the analysis tree and thus the constituent structure in full view, the remaining exercises hide or change parts of it. The student has at his disposal yet more new commands, with which he can add and connect nodes.

F) Show partial tree, ask for reconstruction

In the exercises discussed so far the student only has to label constituents, which have already been grouped together. In this exercise he has to put the parts into the right combinations himself. In the selected tree some nodes and connections are removed. The student has to reconstruct the tree (see fig. 9). New commands in this exercise are I (Insert) to add nodes to the partial tree and T (Tie) to connect a father with a son. New nodes must be inserted from a node already in the tree and they are immediately connected to that node. The T command can then be used to add the other connections from the new node. In the example of fig. 9 the first operation could be to insert a new node as the father of the node marked

-7- and then to connect the new node to the nodes marked -5- and -6-, thus creating a noun phrase node dominating 'THE', 'LITTLE' and 'SQUARE'. At every operation the student is told whether it is correct or not and only correct operations have an effect on the tree. Therefore, only correct nodes and connections will ever be present in the partial tree.

```
ON THE FAR SIDE OF THE LITTLE SQUARE THERE WAS A WALL WITH A PIERCED DECORATIVE
            ┌──1─ . . . . . . . . .  ON
            │                -5- .  THE
     ┌──1───┤                -6- .  FAR
     │      │                -7- .  SIDE
     │      └─(2)-           -8- .  OF
     │                       -9- .  THE
     │                       -a- .  LITTLE
 -*──┤                       -b- .  SQUARE
     ├──2- . . . . . . . . . . . .  THERE
     ├──3- . . . . . . . . . . . .  WAS
     │      ┌──1- . . . . . . . . .  A
     │      ├──2- . . . . . . . . .  WALL
     └──4───┤      ┌──1- . . . . . .  WITH
            │      │      ┌──1- . . .  A
            └──3───┤      ├──2- . . .  PIERCED
                   └──2───┼──3- . . .  DECORATIVE
                          ├──4- . . .  BORDER
                          └──5───┬──1- .  IN
                                 └──2- .  BRICKWORK.

PREPOSITIONAL COMPLEMENT:NOUN PHRASE
command:
scroll:YUDLR<>() focus:FS1-9OPNMJ exer:QAIC view:V help:? exit:X
```

Figure 9: Reconstruct the tree

H) Show incorrect tree, ask for correction

In the analysis tree one or more correct labels or connections are altered and the student has to spot the errors and correct them (see fig. 11). In this exercise one more command is introduced. E (Erase) can be used to erase a node or connection. As we start with an incorrect tree and do not know every possible path from this incorrect tree to the correct one, it is not possible to react to every operation. The student can be told if he is right only when he feels that he has finished correcting the tree.

G) Show partial tree and labelling, ask for reconstruction

This exercise combines labelling as in exercise D with tree reconstruction as in exercise F. The student now has to provide the entire analysis of the part removed from the tree (see fig. 10). In an extreme form of this exercise, the student can be asked to provide a complete analysis of the utterance.

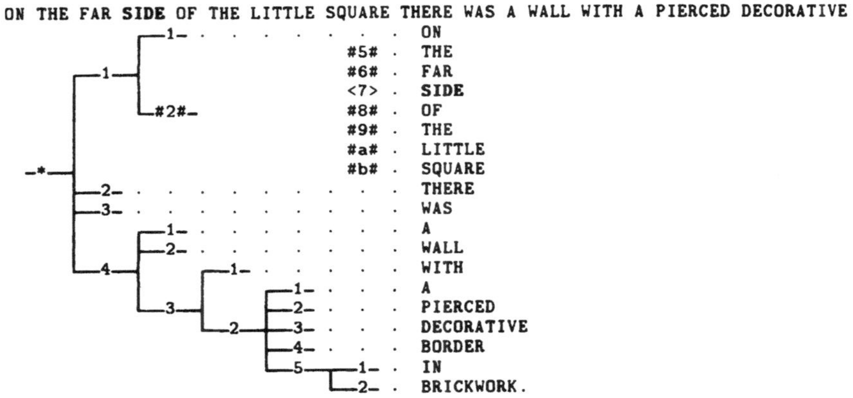


```
???:???
command:
scroll:YUDLR<>() focus:FS1-9OPNMJ exer:QAICO view:V help:? exit:X
```

Figure 10: Reconstruct the tree and the labelling

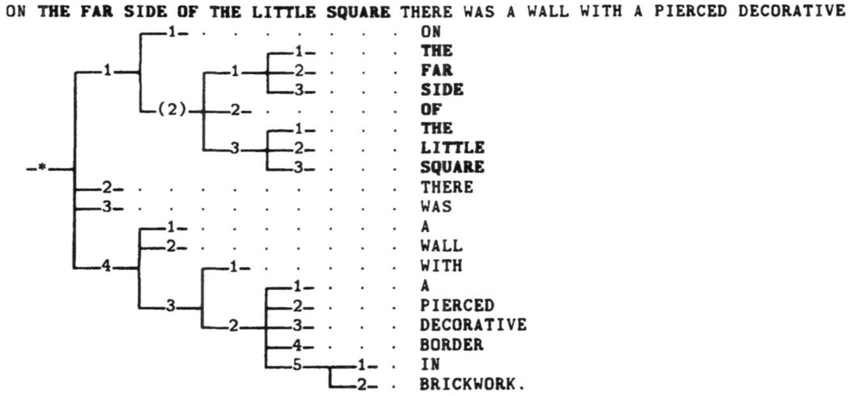


```
PREPOSITIONAL COMPLEMENT:COORDINATION
command:
scroll:YUDLR<>() focus:FS1-9OPNMJ exer:QAICEO view:V help:? exit:X
```

Figure 11: Correct the tree and the labelling

3. PROBLEMS TO BE SOLVED

The list above indicates exercises in the CLUES system that may prove useful. There are, however, some problems yet to be solved before these ideas can become reality.

3.1 Selection procedure

The selection procedure as it is currently used in the Linguistic Database will have to undergo some changes. Merely indicating an interesting pattern is not enough. Not only the type of exercise will have to be indicated, but also which nodes, labels and connections have to be hidden or altered. Exercises A to E can be handled in a straightforward way, F and G are manageable, but exercise H will be especially problematic in this respect.

Another problem in selection is the need to weed out utterances which, although they contain the structure to be exercised, also contain, in another part of the tree, something which must not be shown to the student. This could be a problematic construct which the student will only learn about later in the course and which at the moment will only confuse him. This weeding out can either be done by extra specifications in the pattern or, probably better, by having special, restricted corpora for the different stages of the course.

3.2 Choice of Grammar

A similar problem has to do with the question of what grammar should be used. The formal grammar used in the (automated) syntactic analysis of a corpus (Keulen 1986, Oostdijk 1984) is very different from the grammar presented to students in a syntax course (Aarts and Aarts 1982). For example, while student grammars restrict themselves to phrasal and clausal coordination, accounting for coordination of incomplete phrases by postulating some kind of ellipsis, a formal grammar cannot deal with coordination in this way and will have to describe it at all constituent levels. This necessitates some changes in the analysis trees so that they become suitable for use by students. In most cases renaming and removing labels will be sufficient, but there may be constructs which require rebuilding part of the tree.

3.3 Reactions to the student's answers

As long as the student answers all questions correctly, it is sufficient to say 'Well done!', but what should the reaction to failure be? Of course, it is possible to say 'Wrong' and let the student try until he arrives at the correct answer or to give the correct answer after the first try. From a pedagogical point of view, however, neither of these techniques are valid options. The least one can do is to give a hint after a certain number of failures. Giving hints is, unfortunately, not a straightforward matter. It assumes an understanding of the correct answer and, what is more problematic, insight into the error made by the student. Both of these are hindered by the fact that the exact sentence under consideration is unknown to the teacher when he creates the exercise. A simple hint may be built in, but can completely miss the point if the student makes a different error than the one anticipated by the teacher. Aid in the development of exercises will be provided by the inclusion of a logbook function, which monitors the actions of the student, so that they can be analysed later on.

What is also to be determined on the basis of the student's answer is the next task to be performed. Should the same exercise be done with a new utterance or can the student proceed to another exercise, and if so, which one? Again, we will need to understand what the student is doing. In the case of tertiary education we can assume that the student has enough insight into the matter to decide for himself if he wants to do the same exercise again or go on to the next one. If the system is to be used more widely, however, a scoring mechanism will have to be added, which can be used to make this decision for him.

Building into the system reactions that actually take into account the precise nature of student answers brings us very near the realm of artificial intelligence, which is far beyond the scope of the CLUES project.

4. CONCLUSION

A system like CLUES can be a very valuable instrument in training students in the practical use of grammar. The possibility of focussing exercises on particular aspects of the grammatical domain, combined with a large set of example utterances makes the system a powerful tool. The latter property distinguishes the system from the other syntax teaching programs presented in this volume by Pankhurst, Huiskens and Coppen, and Robat, which have a small set of built-in sentences. The variety of exercise material and the fact that it is taken from actual language use will have such a positive effect on student motivation that we feel it will more than compensate for the disadvantages mentioned.

It must be emphasised that CLUES is no more than an exercising tool. It is not suitable for use as an independent course, as it cannot provide follow-up questions that take the student's reactions into account. CLUES will be viable only in combination with a regular syntax course, but this combination will certainly be more than the sum of its parts.

REFERENCES

Aarts, J. and F. Aarts. 1982. *English Syntactic Structures*, Pergamon Press, Oxford

Keulen, F. 1986. 'The Dutch Computer Corpus Pilot Project', in Aarts, J. and W. Meijs (eds.) *Corpus Linguistics II*, Rodopi, Amsterdam

Oostdijk, N. 1984. 'An Extended Affix Grammar for the English Noun Phrase', in Aarts, J. and W. Meijs (eds.) *Corpus Linguistics I*, Rodopi, Amsterdam

Van Halteren, H. and N. Oostdijk. 1988. 'Using an Analysed Corpus as a Linguistic Database', in Roper, J. (vol. ed.) Hamesse, J. and A. Zampolli (ser. eds.) *Computers in Literary and Linguistic Computing*, Proceedings of the XIIIth ALLC Conference (Norwich 1986)

Van Halteren, H. and Th. van den Heuvel. (forthcoming). *Linguistic Exploitation of Syntactic Databases*, Rodopi, Amsterdam

APPENDIX I: List of Abbreviations in Figures

Function labels:

AD	adverbial
CP	prepositional complement
DET	determiner
HD	head
POM	postmodifier
PREM	premodifier
PRP	preposition
PRSU	provisional subject
UTT	utterance
VB	verb

Category labels:

AJ	adjective
DE	determiner
ETH	existential there
NO	noun
NP	noun phrase
PP	prepositional phrase
PREP	preposition
SF	finite sentence
VCOF	copula finite

Search Pattern keywords:

CAT	category
FUN	function
SNO	son number
WOR	word(s)
WCT	word count

APPENDIX II: List of Commands

Y	yank screen so as to show focus
U/D	scroll screen or offspring up/down
L/R	scroll screen or attributes left/right
</>	scroll sentence left/right
(/)	scroll focus left/right
F	move focus to father
S	move focus to son

1...9	move focus to son no. 1...9	
O	move focus to last son	
P	move focus to previous brother	
N	move focus to next brother	
M	focus on marked node	
	F	towards father
	P	towards previous brothers
	N	towards next brothers
	S	towards son
B	jump to orphaned branch	
J	jump focus to node	
	F	node with specified function
	C	node with specified category
	A	node with specified affix
	W	leaf with specified word
	R	repetition of previous jump
Q	repeat the question	
C	is exercise complete?	
A	give the correct answer	
G	go to next exercise in series	
O	open node to answer a question	
H	requested node is here	
I	insert a node	
	F	as father of the focus
	S	as son of the focus
	P	as previous brother of the focus
	N	as next brother of the focus
T	tie orphaned branch as son to focus	
E	erase the focus	
V	go to other view	
?	provide help info, i.e. show this screen	
X	choose from extra command list	

Commands may be prefixed by a parameter. This parameter consists of a hash (#) followed by a number. Alternatively, an asterisk (*) may be used as an abbreviation of a hash followed by the maximum number relevant in a particular context. In case no parameter is given, a default value of one is assumed.

Software list

1. GENERAL PACKAGES

– FRAMEWORK	Ashton-Tate
– AppleWorks	Apple
– Knowledge Man	Contact: J. Rézeau Rue da la Joussemelière 31 85170 Dompierre/Yon France
– Symphony	Lotus Development Corporation
– Turbo Lightning Package	Borland International

2. CONCORDANCE PROGRAMS

– COCO	Contact: T. Johns University of Birmingham P.O. Box 363 Birmingham B15 2TT England
– KWIC	Contact: T. Johns
– Micro-Concord	Contact: T. Johns
– Wordcruncher	ETC 5600 North University Avenue Provo, Utah 84604 U.S.A.

3. DATABASE PROGRAMS

– dBase II	Ashton-Tate
– dBase III	Ashton-Tate
– LDB	TOSCA Workgroup Erasmusplein 1 6525 HT Nijmegen The Netherlands

– Lotus 1-2-3	Lotus Development Corporation

4. WORD PROCESSORS

– ABC	Acornsoft Ltd 4a Market Hill Cambridge England
– Spellbinder	Ebing Data Systems Ede The Netherlands
– WordPerfect	WP Corporation Orem, Utah U.S.A.
– WordStar	MicroPro International Corporation

5. CALL PROGRAMS

– ALEXIS	Wolters-Noordhoff B.V. P.O. Box 58 9700 MB Groningen The Netherlands
– AMOR	Stichting L.O.C. Groesbeekseweg 30 6524 DC Nijmegen The Netherlands
– Camelot	Computer-Based International Development and Research 11011 South West, 104th Street Miami, Florida 33176-3393 U.S.A.
– CASA	Department of English Grote Kruisstraat 2/I 9712 TS Groningen The Netherlands
– Clozemaster	Wida Software 2 Nicholas Gardens London England

– Developing Tray	ILECC John Ruskin Street London England
– Domesday	BBC – Acorn – Philips Open Universiteit (Marlies Bitter) 045 – 762222
– Gapkit	Camsoft 7 Roman Drive Leeds England
– Loan	Listing in Higgins, J. and T. Johns (1984) *Computers in Language Learning*, London
– London Adventure	Cambridge University Press
– Storyboard	Wida Software 2 Nicholas Gardens London England
– TAIGA	University of Twente P.O. Box 217 7500 AE Enschede The Netherlands
– VOCAL	Department of English Grote Kruisstraat 2/I 9712 TS Groningen The Netherlands
– ZICOM	Stichting L.O.C. Groesbeekseweg 30 6524 DC Nijmegen The Netherlands

Author Index

Aarts, F., 109, 110., 157
Aarts, J., 109, 110, 157
Abercrombie, J., 18
Allen, J., 43
Anandam, K., 85

Breen, M., 40, 43
Bright, J., 44
Brumfit, C., 42
Burt, M., 14

Candlin, C., 43, 88
Cooke, D., 37
Coppen, P.-A., 7, 158

Dakin, J., 14
Davies, F., 10
Dudley-Evans, A., 12
Dulay, H., 14

Edmonson, W., 93
Ek, J. van, 53, 137

Foulds, D., 19
Fowler, H., 25

Gray, P., 45
Griswold, R., 120

Halteren, H. van, 7, 147
Hardisty, D., 5, 37,42
Heuvel, Th. van den, 147
Hewer, S., 44, 45
Higgins, J., 12, 93
Hockey, S., 18
Huiskens, L., 7, 158

Jansen, C., 75
Johns, T., 5, 6, 9, 10, 11, 12, 15, 24, 43, 93

Kelly, L., 13
Keulen, F., 157
King, P., 20
Krashen, S., 42, 43

Leech, G., 55, 88
Lesgold, A., 85
Looijmans, P., 6, 75

Maat, K., 75
McGregor, G., 44

Oostdijk, N., 147, 157

Pankhurst, J. 6, 158
Papert, S., 94
Phillips, M. 13, 36, 40
Pilot, A., 75
Poage, J., 120
Polonski, I. 120

Renouf, A., 20
Rézeau, J., 6, 18, 42
Robat, N., 7, 137, 158
Roe, P., 40
Ruyssevelt, F. van, 5

Schrauwen, D., 75
Seifert, C., 6
Self, J., 87
Seliger, J., 14
Sinclair, J., 20
Sleutjes, A., 6
Smith, F., 11
Steehouder, M., 75
Stone, R., 37

Widdowson, H., 42
Willis, D., 20
Willis, J., 20
Windeatt, S., 6, 42

Yang, H., 25, 26

List of Contributors

Theo Bongaerts
Department of Applied Linguistics
University of Nijmegen
Erasmusplein 1
6525 HT Nijmegen
The Netherlands

Peter-Arno Coppen
Department of Dutch
University of Nijmegen
Erasmusplein 1
6525 HT Nijmegen
The Netherlands

Pieter de Haan
Department of English
University of Nijmegen
Erasmusplein 1
6525 HT Nijmegen
The Netherlands

Hans van Halteren
Department of English
University of Nijmegen
Erasmusplein 1
6525 HT Nijmegen
The Netherlands

David Hardisty
Rua Augusto Gil 152[E]
1000 Lisboa
Portugal

Lucy Huiskens
Océ Nederland BV
Research & Development
P.O. Box 101
5900 MA Venlo
The Netherlands

Tim Johns
University of Birmingham
P.O. Box 363
Birmingham B15 2TT
England

Sylvia Lobbe
Teacher Training College Zuidwest-Nederland
P.O. Box 2967
2601 CZ Delft
The Netherlands

Paul Looymans
Dept. of Management, Organization and Personnel
Nijenrode, The Netherlands School of Business
Straatweg 25
3621 BG Breukelen
The Netherlands

James Pankhurst
Department of Germanic Languages
Cluster Trans-binnenstad
Trans 14
3512 JK Utrecht
The Netherlands

Joseph Rézeau
Rue da la Joussemelière 31
85170 Dompierre/Yon
France

Nico Robat
Department of English
University of Groningen
Grote Kruisstraat 2/I
9712 TS Groningen
The Netherlands

Frank van Ruyssevelt
Teacher Training College Sittard
Oude Markt 5
6130 AN Sittard
The Netherlands

Carla Seiffert
Dept. of Applied Linguistics
Nijenrode, The Netherlands School of Business
Straatweg 25
3621 BG Breukelen
The Netherlands

Albert Sleutjes
Teacher Training College Sittard
Oude Markt 5
6130 AN Sittard
The Netherlands

Marlies Smit
Hainerweg 30
6072 Dreieich-Götzen Hain
F.R.G.

Herman Wekker
Department of English
University of Groningen
Grote Kruisstraat 2/I
9712 TS Groningen
The Netherlands

Scott Windeatt
Institute for English Language Education
Bowland College
University of Lancaster
Lancaster OA1 4YR
England